MURDER C.O.D.

The ringing of the doorbell awoke her. Alice McArthur walked up to the foyer in bare feet and peeked through the peephole to find a man standing there holding a flower arrangement and clipboard in one hand and a pen in the other. Alice smiled to herself as she opened the door. She took the pen, but he was hesitant to give her the clipboard.

Something snapped in Alice's mind. For a split second she looked into the man's eyes, and what she saw frightened her. Suddenly, she knew why he was there. She turned and ran upstairs, and as she reached the end of the upstairs hallway, a bullet whizzed past her ears, slamming into the sheetrock.

She screamed as the explosion reverberated through the house, and headed for the bedroom. She darted into the closet in a desperate attempt to hide. He neared the open closet door and for a brief moment, their eyes met. . . .

MURDER IN LITTLE ROCK

formerly titled
BOUQUET FOR MURDER

Jan Meins

ST. MARTIN'S PRESS/NEW YORK

This book is dedicated with love to Tom, Christie and Bobby for their understanding and patience and to Lora for making us all laugh.

This book was formerly published by Rose Publishing Co. under the title *Bouquet for Murder*.

MURDER IN LITTLE ROCK

Copyright © 1987 by Jan Meins.

Library of Congress Catalog Card Number: 87-063216

ISBN: 0-312-92025-3   Can. ISBN: 0-312-92024-5

Printed in the United States of America

Rose Publishing edition published 1987
First St. Martin's Press mass market edition/January 1990

10 9 8 7 6 5 4 3 2 1

PROLOGUE

This book is the result of three years of research—specifically examination of newspaper clippings, hundreds of pages of court and police records, and tape-recorded interviews with more than eighty people intimately familiar with Alice McArthur and what happened in Little Rock, Arkansas, on a hot day in July, 1982.

In a few instances, events have been reconstructed, as in Chapter 1. These reconstructions, however, are based upon compelling evidence.

Chapter One

EUGENE JAMES "YANKEE" HALL HAULED dope for a living, but he had used so much of it his brain was fried. He thought of himself as a lady's man, and although, at forty-three, he could be considered middle-aged, he didn't see himself that way. His newest girlfriend was Mary "Lee" Orsini, a pretty brunette whom he had gotten into bed early in their relationship, and as a result of their intimacy, she told him about an opportunity to make some quick, easy money so they could go into the cocaine business together.

She said all they had to do was kill the wife of Bill McArthur, a Little Rock lawyer who was willing to pay $25,000 to have the job done. The lawyer's wife, Alice, was threatening to leave him, take the kids, and ruin his law practice. If Hall could get the job done before the Fourth of July weekend, the lawyer would add an extra five grand.

"It's this lawyer's wife. She's giving him trouble, you know, and he's willing to pay good for getting rid of her," Hall told his black friend, Larry Darnell McClendon. "All you gotta do is act like you're a delivery man. I'll supply the gun and drive the car."

Hall and McClendon, twenty-seven, had been friends for years, despite the difference in their races. Sometimes they even shared the same toothbrush, and they had been in and out of jail together several times. But Hall didn't trust McClendon enough to tell him who hired them or about the brunette or about the

$25,000. "After expenses, your share will be $6,000," Hall told McClendon.

Lee Orsini told Hall that Alice's children would be away at camp the first week in July, and the job had to be done then. She gave him a floral delivery sign to put in his car window, a clipboard filled with a phony list of deliveries, and she wrote the lawyer's wife's name in one of the columns so he and McClendon could pose as delivery men.

On the morning of Friday, July 2, 1982, Yankee Hall left his apartment in downtown Little Rock and drove across the Arkansas River to a garage and wrecker service in North Little Rock. He used McClendon's car, a 1970 Cadillac, to pick up the clipboard and sign he had left in a Corvette he had been driving until the motor gave out the day before. The Corvette was one of many cars Hall had worked on while doing odd jobs for a local mechanic.

On the way back from the wrecking yard, Hall stopped at a Magic Mart discount store in North Little Rock and called the lawyer's home. There was no answer, so he drove back to his apartment. From his apartment, he called Orsini to see if she knew when the lawyer's wife would be home. She said all she knew was the lawyer and his wife were supposed to leave for Hot Springs, a nearby resort area, that afternoon. "She might be out shopping. Be patient," Orsini said. "She'll be home, and she'll be alone."

McClendon left Hall's apartment and went to his mother's house for lunch. A short time later Hall went to a Gulf station and telephoned the lawyer's residence. It was about 2 p.m. when he got an answer.

"Hello," a woman said.

"Is John Allen there?" he asked.

Alice McArthur was glad she and her husband had sent the children away to camp. She wasn't the kind of mother who liked to ship her kids off, but this summer camp for the children had given her and her husband a chance to get to know each other again. She didn't even mind joining friends at the lake in Hot Springs for the weekend because she and Bill had enjoyed the last four nights alone, and now it was time to share some fun with their best friends.

Alice planned to go to the lake with one of her girl-friends that Friday, but sometime during the morning, she decided against leaving without her husband. She would call him later and tell him of her decision to wait for him.

Alice McArthur was a nice-looking woman who could have easily passed for several years younger than her true age, forty-one. She was tan and athletic and wore her hair frosted, which complemented her blue eyes. She kept in shape by playing tennis, and after her husband left for work that morning, she prepared to go to the Westside Tennis & Fitness Club, a private facility that boasted both indoor and outdoor courts.

She closed up the house, opened the door of her Oldsmobile Cutlass and slid behind the wheel but hesitated before turning on the ignition. Several weeks earlier someone had planted a bomb beneath the car, below the driver's seat, and when Alice started her car one morning, the bomb partially detonated. She was lucky; she only sustained scratches to one leg, and her car was just slightly damaged.

The police suspected the bombing might have something to do with a nightclub her husband owned, and they said it would have ripped both Alice and her car apart had it detonated properly. Alice realized how fortunate she was to be alive, and she hoped the police would soon solve the case. Both she and her husband assumed the bomb was meant for him, although the police had no firm suspects. Immediately after the bombing, she was tense and nervous and had expressed her feelings to her closest friends, but time was working its magic and calming her fears, and Alice was beginning to relax her guard.

Alice started the car and maneuvered it through the tree-lined streets of her neighborhood, Pleasant Valley, which sits on the hilly western outskirts of Little Rock, the capital of Arkansas and its financial, medical, media and cultural center. Little Rock has many fine neighborhoods. The finest, perhaps, is Edgehill, a cluster of hillside mansions that fetch up to one million dollars each. Pleasant Valley, which many real estate salespersons claim is Edgehill's main competitor, is where many of the town's professionals live. It has a fine country club, and many Pleasant Valley children attend private schools. Alice's children, Robyn, 12, and Chuck, 7, attended a Catholic school, not because Alice wanted to keep up with the neighbors, but because Alice was Catholic. Swimming pools are scattered throughout the area—Alice and Bill McArthur had one, too—and all the homes have well-manicured lawns and two- and three-car garages. Many Pleasant Valley homes have housekeepers, but Alice was too practical to waste money on a housekeeper. Perhaps her Cajun background made her that way, for she saw no need to hire a housekeeper when she could take care of things herself.

As Alice approached the tennis club, she realized the day was already becoming dull with heat and humidity, and she hoped to get in a few games before it got too hot. But she learned her league had been canceled, so she decided to spend the rest of the sultry morning shopping. Sometime during her shopping trip, she stopped at a boutique, called the Birdcage, where her friend Mary Bass worked. Mary ran over and hugged her.

"How's your leg?" Mary asked, referring to the injuries Alice sustained when her car was bombed.

"I'll tell you one thing, it's smaller than yours," Alice said. She kidded Mary because Mary had put on weight, and that was Alice's way of encouraging her friend to start a diet.

Mary showed her some new T-shirts: "This green one would be pretty on you."

"You know what, Mary, I don't really need one, I've got so many things."

"So you're finally admitting it!" Mary said. She had been teasing Alice for a long time about having more clothes than she would ever wear.

Mary asked Alice about the bombing, but Alice said she wasn't supposed to talk about it. Alice held her thumb and forefinger up to indicate an inch and said, "I think they are that close to getting them." Alice led Mary to believe that Pulaski County Sheriff Tommy Robinson was about to crack the case.

"If anybody can get them, Tommy can," Mary said. Alice agreed.

Alice told her about the plans for the weekend and the children being away at camp. She also told Mary how much she and her husband, Bill, had been enjoying themselves and named all the places he had taken her to eat during the last few days. The two women joked about it because Alice was always putting her husband on a diet.

"I'll bet Bill is thinking he has died and gone to Heaven!" Mary said, and Alice laughed.

Before Alice left the store, she told Mary she had decided to stay in town to wait for her husband. She would drive to the lake with him after he closed the club. Although he had a partner in his club, BJ's Star Studded Honky Tonk, tonight was his turn to close up.

Alice stopped by the grocery store before returning home and picked up ingredients for red beans and rice, one of her favorite dishes from her Cajun background and one she intended to make for her friends at the lake that weekend. When she arrived back home, she parked her car in the drive and took all her packages into the house. She separated the things she wanted to take to the lake and left those sacks just inside the front door for her husband to pack into the car later. Her husband called her a little after 12:30, and she told him about the two new pairs of shorts she had bought for him and her decision to wait and drive to Hot Springs with him.

"If they don't fit, I want to take them back and exchange them before the store closes, because I've decided to wait and drive to the lake with you," she said.

"Fine, Hon, I'll get home as soon as I can. We can leave from the club tonight, or drive up in the morning. . . ."

"Sounds good. The store closes at 5:30, so be sure to get home in time to try on the shorts. I can exchange them today if they don't fit."

Alice hung up the receiver, grabbed her cigarettes and lighter, which were sitting on the bar in the kitchen, and the portable phone, went downstairs to the family room and turned on the television. About 2:16 the phone rang. She picked it up. "Hello."

"Is John Allen there?" a man asked.

"You must have the wrong number," she said, thinking it strange she had received a couple of hang-up calls since getting back from shopping—and now a wrong number. But she wasn't too worried about it because she knew the telephone company had put a trap on her phone since the bombing. The device "trapped" incoming calls and enabled the telephone company to trace where the calls were coming from. She also kept a tape recorder near the telephone and recorded every call. If a caller turned out to be a friend, she would turn the recorder off.

She laid the phone on the table, sat back on the couch, propped up her feet and relaxed.

Yankee Hall telephoned Larry McClendon at his mother's house and asked him to pick him up at his apartment. When he arrived, Hall got into the passenger side and shut the door, but when McClendon turned the key, the Cadillac wouldn't start.

Hall looked under the hood and discovered a burned wire, which he soon replaced. But when he tried to start the car again, he realized the battery was now run down. Hall walked to the nearby apartment of his friend, Mike Willingham, a Little Rock policeman. He borrowed Willingham's pickup, went to a gas station and bought a new battery for McClendon's car, then drove back to his apartment in Willingham's truck.

While Hall and McClendon were replacing the battery, Lee Orsini drove by. McClendon was busy under the hood of the car and didn't notice Hall waving to her that everything was all right. She nodded and drove off. About 3:30 p.m., they finally got McClendon's car started and took off for Pleasant Valley, Hall in the pickup and McClendon in the Cadillac. A few miles from their destination, Hall pulled the truck over and McClendon pulled beside him.

"I left the damn apartment door open at my place," Hall said. "You go shut it and lock it while I get the flowers, and I'll meet you on the west side of Interstate 430. I'll pull over on the shoulder and wait for you."

Hall stopped at a flower shop, bought a centerpiece of colorful springtime flowers, and picked out a card that said, "Have a nice day." Then he went to the Interstate to wait for McClendon.

It didn't take long for McClendon to get back. Hall put the gun, a .38-caliber Smith and Wesson, into McClendon's car along with the flower arrangement, clipboard and floral delivery sign. They left the truck parked on the shoulder of the Interstate and drove in the Cadillac to the Christ The King Catholic Church parking lot, on the edge of Pleasant Valley. There, they took the license plate off the car and placed the hand-made sign in the back window. Hall took over the driving while McClendon checked the gun. "Once you go in, I'll kind of get out of the car, and when I hear, you know, when I hear the shot, I'll go in and make sure everything is all right," he told McClendon.

McClendon clutched the gun nervously, wrapped it in a towel and nodded.

The ringing of the doorbell and the barking of Alice's toy poodle awoke her. The television was still on as she pulled herself up from the sofa, wondering who could be at the door. She thought it might be her friend, Beth, and for a moment, she wished she had a "Do Not Disturb" sign hanging out front.

She walked up to the foyer in bare feet and peeked through the peephole to find a black man standing there holding a flower arrangement and clipboard in one hand and a pen in the other. Alice smiled to herself as she opened the wooden door, then the glass storm door, thinking how nice it was for her husband to send her flowers—and for no special occasion— just like newlyweds.

The black man held the door open with his back and handed Alice the bouquet. She smiled and told him how pretty the flowers were. She took the pen in her left hand, but he was hesitant to give her the clipboard.

Something snapped in Alice's mind. For a split second she looked into the man's eyes, and what she saw frightened her. Suddenly, she knew why he was there. It took only a moment for Alice's athletic body to react. As she turned and ran upstairs, her only thought was to get to the pistol her husband kept on the shelf in their bedroom closet, but the faster she tried to run, the heavier her feet felt. She dared not look back, for she knew he was close behind her, and as she reached the end of the upstairs hallway, a bullet whizzed past her ears, slamming into the grasscloth and sheetrock. She screamed as the explosion reverberated through the house, and she turned off to the right, entering her bedroom. Now she couldn't remember why she headed for the bedroom, and she panicked. She ran blindly toward the closet.

She darted into the closet, overturning a footstool, and clawed at some jeans hanging above her in a desperate attempt to hide herself. By the time he fired a second shot, which again missed her, Alice had collapsed to the floor. He neared the open closet door and for a brief moment their eyes met. Alice turned her head and covered her face with her hands and prayed words lost in her mind before they were formed.

Joyce Gudmondson had noticed the strange-looking men at the house across the street. She wasn't nosey, but everyone in the neighborhood was more alert since the bombing. Joyce first saw them when she went out to the garage where she kept her washing machine. A load of throw rugs had gotten tangled together on one side of the washer and thrown the machine off balance. While she was rearranging the rugs, she heard a pop and decided some children must be shooting off their Fourth of July fireworks already. People in Pleasant Valley knew this was all they would hear for the next three nights: constant crackles and pops and sirens as firemen went about putting out fires caused by runaway skyrockets and Roman candles. She glanced back over at the house across the street and saw the driver of the old Cadillac get out and walk up to the front door. Finishing her work, she closed the washing machine lid and was about to go inside to call Alice when she heard a car start up. Looking back across the street again, she saw the old car driving away with a white man behind the wheel and a black man on the passenger side.

Jesus, this is hard...I have laid in bed thinking about this, it took me awhile after this to start envi-

sioning what happened there that day. The sheer terror that she went through for awhile is almost more than I can bear to think about—I would have given my life for her. That's easy to say, not so easy to do, but I never got that opportunity....

... William C. "Bill" McArthur, 1984

Chapter Two

MARY MYRTLE HATCHER EDGED CLOSER to the frog. She sat down Indian-style and rested her BB gun over her knees, watching the frog. A breeze caught her hair. She took a deep breath and let it out quietly so as not to disturb her frog. He really wasn't her frog, but since spotting him a few minutes earlier, she had claimed him for her own. If he got too near the lake, she would grab him quickly. She knew if he plopped into the muddy water, she would never be able to catch him. A bluejay squawked overhead, and Mary waited. Listening by the lake, she could hear all kinds of birds, even the distant drilling of a wood-pecker. She picked a puff ball and waited for a good, strong breeze. When it came, she puckered up and blew hard and smiled as the feathery seeds drifted away. The sun was making the top of her head hot.

"Oh, boy! A toad!"

The girl turned and saw her little brother running toward the frog. She hadn't noticed him until he was too close.

"It's not a toad, it's a frog, it can swim," she said. "Get away, you're scaring it."

"I'm gonna shoot it," her brother said, raising his BB gun to his shoulder.

"If you shoot my frog, I'll shoot you," she threatened.

"You will not. Mama would beat the daylights out of you."

It happened quickly. The boy shot the frog, and his sister did just as she had promised. She shot him, right in the leg.

"I'm gonna tell," he cried.

"Go ahead you little crybaby. Mama won't believe you anyway," said Mary.

Mary Myrtle Hatcher was born August 17, 1947, in Searcy, Arkansas. She was thirteen months older than her brother, Ron, and from the time she was old enough to walk, she fought with him—real fights and bruises and bloody noses, and most of the time, because she was bigger, she won.

Their father, a cattleman from Houston, was an alcoholic. He used to get drunk and threaten his wife and older daughter, Frances, with a shotgun. They would cry and fuss and holler and run away, not coming back home until they were sure he was in one of his sound, drunk sleeps. When Henry Hatcher died of cancer at the age of fifty-two, Ron was two years old, and Mary was three.

The Hatchers lived in an old farmhouse on 100 acres of land near the back gate of the Little Rock Air Force Base, a few miles north of the twin cities of Little Rock and North Little Rock. The Hatchers had owned 600 acres but sold off some of the land until they wound up with only one-sixth of their original holdings. The acreage left had three lakes, one small one and two large ones covering about eighty-five acres, and over the years, the lakes became known as Hatcher Lakes. Although life wasn't easy for the Hatcher kids, Ron loved the land, but the Hatcher homestead held no charm for Mary, and she couldn't wait until the day she could leave home.

They raised cattle. Ron and one hired man took care of the livestock, and his mother, Julia Hatcher, planted a large garden each spring. In the summer she sold vegetables, and in the fall she canned vegetables to stock their pantry for winter.

Since they lived in a large house and owned land, nobody suspected the Hatchers were poor, but they were. Mrs. Hatcher, who had only a sixth-grade education, worked nine months each year as a school bus driver and in the school cafeteria. She was too proud to take charity.

Mrs. Hatcher was strict and gave her children the impression she didn't like men, and she did not spare the rod. Although she didn't talk ill of the children's dead father in front of them, Ron could sense her bitterness toward him. Ron felt that his father had not been the type of man who was easy to love. He thought of his father as a hard man, and his mother once let it slip that his father had killed a man in Texas.

Ron often thought of his mother as hard too, and while he wanted to be a good son, his feelings toward her were all mixed up, and he grew to resent her strict discipline.

By the time Ron was in the eighth grade, he caught up with Mary physically. One day after school when the two got into an argument, Mary tried to shove him; and, finally, Ron decided he had all he was going to take from his sister. He slapped her face, knocking her across the kitchen. After that they still fought, but Mary became much more cunning.

Mary quit school at the age of sixteen and on December 22, 1963 married Douglas Sudbury, a twenty-one-year-old Kentuckian who was an airman at the Little Rock Air Force Base. Shortly afterward the couple divorced but remarried on July 14, 1966. They moved to Riverside, California, and Mary gave birth to a daughter she named Tiffany LaVergene.

Not long after Mary left, Ron agreed to sell the Hatcher farmland, a move he later regretted. But at the time it seemed sensible. A smaller house in town seemed to be in his mother's best interest; it would be a lot less worry for her. Besides, Ron had a job with an engineering firm out of town and would be moving as soon as he graduated from high school.

Mr. Hatcher had left the 100 acres to Ron, Mary and Mrs. Hatcher in equal shares, but Mrs. Hatcher had a lifetime dowry in it. She could live on it, but she couldn't sell it without her children's approval. In 1968, when Ron was eighteen years old, he signed the papers agreeing to the sale of the house, and with the proceeds, Mrs. Hatcher purchased a home at 31 Shoshoni Drive in North Little Rock. The payments were low, about $150 per month.

In 1967 Mary Hatcher had divorced Douglas Sudbury for the second time, and by the time Tiffany was two years old, Mary moved back to Arkansas to live with her mother and brother, and Ron's problems began all over again. They quarreled constantly, and Mary always sought to win her mother over to her side of the argument.

Ron had graduated from high school by this time and entered night school at the University of Arkansas at Little Rock. During the day, he worked as a bank teller. Before leaving for work one morning, not long after Mary's return, he and Mary had another argument, but this one was a little worse than usual and almost came to blows.

Later in the day, the bank's president received an anonymous telephone call from a woman who said that Ron Hatcher was involved in drugs.

"I want you to know what kind of boy you have working for you," the caller said. "We were out Saturday night, and Ron was doing drugs and wanted me to do drugs."

The bank official called Ron into his office and confronted him with the information. Ron suspected Mary was behind it and told his boss. Later in the day when the woman called back, Ron's boss allowed him to listen on another phone. There could be no mistake; he knew it was Mary's voice.

Mary Hatcher was employed by the *Arkansas Democrat*, one of the two Little Rock daily newspapers, as a sales representative when she met her second husband, David Raymond May of North Little Rock. They married in 1971, but she walked out on him after six months and resumed the name of Sudbury. After her marriage failed, she held several jobs, including one that took her away during the evenings. She told her brother she was working as a bookkeeper at the Wine Cellar, a Little Rock nightclub.

She was a pretty girl, but she was a little rough around the edges—lacking in social graces found in daughters of the town's professionals. She hadn't been born into the kind of society she longed for, and she intended to change her status in life. The change started by dropping the name, "Mary," and giving herself a new name and a new image. "Lee" was a more suitable moniker for the woman she wanted to be. And the name was only the beginning. She wanted to live in just the right neighborhood, in just the right kind of house. She wanted to be seen in only the right places and shop in the right stores. And she would let nothing stand in her way.

On September 17, 1976, Mary Myrtle Hatcher Sudbury, now twenty-nine, married for a fourth time. Her new husband, a divorcee named Ronald Gary Orsini, was thirty-four and had a daughter from his previous marriage. He was a hard-working man who owned a twenty-five percent interest in a heating and air conditioning business in Little Rock.

Ron Hatcher liked the quiet family man his brother-in-law represented. Ron Orsini enjoyed gun collecting and fishing, and when he wasn't working or fishing, he spent most of his time puttering around the house. He was handy with tools and enjoyed tinkering. Orsini had a shy way of talking, as if he feared he might offend someone. He never acted cross or angry with anyone, including his wife and Tiffany, whom he adopted shortly after the marriage. And Hatcher believed his new brother-in-law truly loved Tiffany. She was a shy little girl who needed a father, and Ron Orsini did the best he could to be a real father to her, Hatcher thought.

Shortly after their marriage the Orsinis purchased a small home in Emerald Gardens Drive in North Little Rock, a town directly across the Arkansas River from Little Rock. North Little Rock is a separate, smaller, less prosperous city, with fewer fancy neighborhoods like Little Rock's Pleasant Valley. Lee Orsini soon concluded the Emerald Gardens Drive house didn't meet her needs nor bring the status she sought for herself, and in July 1980, Metropolitan National Bank loaned the Orsinis $30,000 as down payment for the purchase of an expensive home on Pontiac Drive in a fashionable section of Sherwood, a suburb of North Little Rock. The Orsinis financed the home with a $72,500 loan from Superior Federal Savings.

Mrs. Hatcher's home on Shoshoni was used as collateral for the $30,000, but Ron Hatcher did not know about it.

In 1979 Ron Hatcher became concerned his mother might not be keeping enough insurance on the small home on Shoshoni and asked her several times about the amount of insurance coverage. He felt she was being evasive, so he insisted on seeing the deed.

The Hatcher children and their mother met at an attorney's office August 21, 1980, and Ron was shown the documents relating to the home on Shoshoni. He saw that on June 10, 1980, his mother had signed the

house over to Ron and Mary "Lee" Orsini for collateral on their loan. Ron Hatcher was furious; he felt his
mother had betrayed him, but his anger soon turned
against his sister. When he walked out of the lawyer's
office, he swore he would never speak to his sister
again.

Lee Orsini liked living in a big house, but she didn't
like not having enough money to buy the things she
wanted, including the type for furnishings she thought
a $100,000 home should have. In 1980 she got a job as
an independent contractor for an advertising firm and
earned $27,000, but by March of the next year she had
earned only $81 in commissions, and Ron netted only
$558 every two weeks from his air conditioning busi-
ness. With mortgage payments of more than $700 a
month, money was tight at the Orsini home.
    The Orsinis opened a savings account at a local sav-
ings and loan in July 1980, but their savings were de-
pleted by September. In November, Lee Orsini
purchased $16,000 worth of Pennsylvania House furni-
ture from Dillard Department Stores, thus increasing
the Orsinis' monthly payments to Dillard's to slightly
more than $900.
    In January 1981 the $30,000 loan from Metropolitan
National Bank, which the Orsinis used to make a down
payment on their Pontiac Drive home was declared
delinquent, and they failed to make their February and
March mortgage payments to Superior Federal. On
March 11, 1981 Lee Orsini called a vice president of
Metropolitan and told her she had just closed the sale
of their old Emerald Gardens home and received
$40,000 cash, and she would now be able to pay the
delinquent note. Despite the banker's insistence that
she bring the money by the bank that afternoon, Mrs.
Orsini said she would wait and bring the money the
next morning.

* * *

On the evening of Wednesday March 11, 1981, Ron Orsini, who was then thirty-eight years old, went to bed alone. His wife had decided to sleep with thirteen-year-old Tiffany, who had been ill for several days. Sometime between 10:30 p.m. and midnight, the house became dark and its occupants quiet. Tiffany's medication helped her relax into a sound sleep. Ron lay on his stomach, one arm above his head, and also fell into a deep sleep on the queen-sized bed decorated with matching sheets and pillow shams of bright, red flowers.

A single gunshot disturbed the quiet on Pontiac Drive sometime before midnight. It took thirty minutes for Ron Orsini to die, as his blood soaked into the flowered print sheets and queen-size mattress. A .38-caliber bullet had entered his body at the crown of his head and traveled through his brain. It exited through his left nostril and came to rest on a pillow.

On the morning Lee Orsini discovered her husband's body, Ron Hatcher received a telephone call from T.J. Farley of the North Little Rock Police Department.

"Are you aware that your brother-in-law was killed last night?" Farley asked.

"My brother-in-law? Which one?" Hatcher exclaimed.

"Ron," Farley replied.

"How?"

"In his bed."

"In his bed!"

"Yes. His wife has accused you of killing him," Farley said.

By the time of Ron's death, the Orsinis' account at Dillard's was sixty days in arrears. The day after Ron's death, Orsini called the vice president of Metropolitan National Bank and said, "They got the money," evidently referring to Orsini's killers and the $40,000 cash she said she had gotten from the sale of the Emerald Gardens home. She also inquired about a credit life insurance policy, but the banker informed her that when the $30,000 note the Orsinis had with the bank became delinquent, the credit life had lapsed. The banker told her to call the abstract company that handled the closing on the Emerald Gardens home and stop payment on the $40,000 check.

"I can't," Orsini said. "They closed in cash."

The banker later learned that the sale of the Emerald Gardens home had been closed there months earlier, and the Orsinis had received a check for only about $7,000 from the sale, plus a second mortgage worth a little more than $11,000.

Ron Orsini had about $75,000 in life insurance plus credit life insurance to pay the mortgage on the Pontiac Drive home in the event of his death. His widow and his former wife waged a court battle over his life insurance, and the court awarded $50,000 of it to his daughter by his previous marriage. Proceeds from the credit life insurance policy paid off the mortgage on the Pontiac Drive home on May 29, 1981.

In the fall of 1981 Metropolitan National Bank foreclosed on Mrs. Hatcher's home at 31 Shoshoni because of the delinquent $30,000 note, Ron Orsini was dead, Ron Hatcher wasn't speaking to his sister, and Lee Orsini seemed to be enjoying the attention the news media gave her husband's death.

Don't believe anything Mary ever says. She can look at you and tell you a lie, and if in any way you suspect it's a lie, she'll tell you another one. If she tells a lie long enough, she begins to believe it.

. . . Ron Hatcher, 1984

Chapter Three

A SMALL TOWN IS LIKE A FAMILY, AND Billy Mac lived in the middle of his, right across the street from the courthouse in Clinton, Arkansas.

The courthouse was the town's heart and the town grew outward from that two-story stone structure, streets and sidewalks reaching like tentacles toward the lush, hilly countryside. Like most Southern county-seat towns, Billy Mac's hometown had been planned in a geometric fashion with the courthouse square as the focal point.

A third-generation descendant of Irish immigrants, Billy Mac grew up around the courthouse square, enjoying the camaraderie and sense of belonging that pervades every aspect of small-town life. As he played and romped through boyhood, he felt a sense of timelessness that comes from seeing the same familiar faces every day, and a sense of security in the knowledge that Clinton was a place where change was slow.

Billy Mac's real name was William Charles McArthur, but it made him feel special when the kids he played with called him by his nickname.

A block away from his home, in front of the courthouse, was a drug store, where the sandy-haired boy spent practically every penny he earned on cherry Cokes, comic books and baseball cards. Next door to the drug store was the one-room law office of Opie Rogers, Billy Mac's best friend.

Rogers had a long, skinny neck, a big Adam's apple,

gray unruly hair, and the ability to earn the trust of children, for he was forthright and honest. He liked Billy Mac and often paid the inquisitive boy to clean up his office and run errands. Billy Mac liked Rogers, too, and although he thought Rogers look like the buzzard in the Heckel and Jeckel cartoons, he admired the odd-looking man and decided when he grew up, he wanted to be a lawyer, just like Rogers.

Billy Mac's father left his job as the manager of an appliance store in 1951 and moved his family 70 miles south to Little Rock, in the center of the state. Billy Mac, then thirteen, thought it surely was the end of the world, or at least the end of his small world of horses, hunting dogs, trips to the swimming hole, summer afternoons at the soda fountain, and good friends he had gone to school with all his life. Billy Mac hated the thought of living in a big city and going to school with strangers. He knew nothing would ever be the same again. But he adjusted to his new life, and after finishing high school, he attended Little Rock Junior College for two years, then spent one year out of school to earn enough money to go back to college.

He enrolled at the University of Arkansas in Fayetteville, a small college town nestled in the foothills of the Ozark Mountains in northwest Arkansas. Fayetteville is a place where the local industry is the university, but also a place that is important to the school's alumni, Arkansas's power brokers. The power brokers in Arkansas are not the hillbillies sometimes associated with the state, although Arkansas has its share of poverty and ignorance. The power brokers operate within a social class known as the good old boys.

Good old boys make their own rules and have a system outsiders might find difficult to understand. You're either born a good old boy or you become one, and once a good old boy, always a good old boy. This designation applies to white males only. A few blacks have entered the mainstream, but they don't wield much power, and they aren't considered members of the good old boy clique. Good old boys are, however, different shapes and sizes—from the three-piece suited banker, businessman, doctor or lawyer to the gentleman farmer who wears cowboy boots, dips Skoal and drives a pickup truck.

A good old boy goes along to get along, and he's tight with the bankers. He knows the proper way of cussing, and he knows how to drawl words like "sombitch" when he wants to distinguish himself from the bluebloods who wouldn't know the first thing about cussing or chewing tobacco. It's rare to find one who is willing to leave the fold, rarer still to find one who will badmouth one of the brethren. In short, good old boys are the ones with money and power, or at least they know the right people to call when they've got a problem. Good old boys can fix anything, from a flat tire to a traffic ticket to a multi-million dollar loan.

Many of the power brokers, the good old boys, send their children to the U of A, to be members of the right fraternity, the same one "Daddy" belonged to when he attended the University and screamed "Woooo Pig Sooooie" at football games. Billy Mac went to the university, too, but he was far from a good old boy. He was the son of a store clerk, neither wealthy nor well-connected.

At Fayetteville, Billy Mac, who now preferred to be called Bill, worked his way through a bachelor's degree by waiting tables at the school cafeteria for a dollar an hour, cutting timber, and taking care of cattle and mending fences on the farms near the school. One year he worked as a houseboy for a sorority in return for free meals and while there he earned the reputation of being a ladies' man. During summer vacations, he lived in Little Rock with his parents and worked as a laborer for a construction company.

He graduated in 1960 and went to work in Little

Rock at the State Rehabilitation Department as a claims examiner. Except for one year in the Army during 1961–62, he worked there until he started law school in 1964.

It was at a college roommate's wedding in 1963 that Bill McArthur met Alice Miller. Alice wasn't excited about the blind date her friend, Mary, had arranged for her. She didn't see anything wrong with going to Mary's wedding alone. Alice was like that. After all, the wedding was going to be in Alice's home town, and she knew practically everybody who was going to be there.

Alice's home was Golden Meadow, Louisiana, 40 miles southwest of New Orleans. Golden Meadow is a small town, built along Bayou LaFourche. The bayou is used by oil barges, tugs and fishing fleets as an avenue to the Gulf of Mexico, and at the time she and Bill met, the town had one main street, Louisiana Highway 1, which runs along the bayou. The town ran back from the highway, only three blocks deep at the most populated part, and you could throw a rock and hit water in almost any direction.

The town is populated mostly by Cajuns, natives of Louisiana descended from French exiles for Canada, a very close-knit, tight-lipped group who don't like or trust outsiders and prefer to be left alone. That's exactly how Alice felt. She didn't like the idea of being paired up with someone who might just turn out to be a bore.

So Alice decided to take along some insurance. She invited a college friend, Jack Davenport, to come home with her for the wedding with the understanding that if her blind date from Arkansas turned out to be a flop, Jack would pretend to be her date.

Alice and Bill met two nights before the wedding at a party in the Rectory Hall of Saint Mark's Catholic Church. She liked what she saw and decided she didn't

need any insurance after all. She was attracted to Bill's
blond hair and blue eyes, and he had a cockiness about
him which intrigued her. He seemed almost arrogant,
but not in an offensive way, and she saw right away
that he was athletic. He liked water skiing and tennis
and horseback riding, and that suited her fine because
she had always been a tomboy.

Bill noticed her too. He liked her healthy, tan athletic appearance. And although others considered her
stride rather masculine, Bill thought it was attractive.
He liked the way Alice had a good time—a little boisterous for most ladies, but genuine, he thought. But
first there was the problem of Jack Davenport. Bill
thought Jack was with Alice so he started flirting with
one of Alice's girlfriends. Alice decided to do something about it.

After the wedding rehearsal, everyone went to a
local restaurant owned by Alice's brother, Leonard.
Bill took some coins from his pocket, walked over to
the juke box and stood there studying the selections.
He punched in his first pick and looked up to find
Alice looking over his shoulder.

"Do you mind if I play some?" she asked.

"No, go ahead," he said.

After making her choices, Bill's first song wound
down and the wheels clicked one of Alice's into place.
She stepped back and looked straight into Bill's eyes.

"Want to dance?" he asked, a little embarrassed at
being forced into asking her.

After a few moments of two-stepping, Alice
abruptly stopped dancing. "You are the most conceited
bastard I ever met," she said.

Bill didn't know what to say and was a little humili-
ated, then angry. He walked off the dance floor and sat
back down at the table and fumed. But in a little while
he began to think it was funny. He cooled off enough
to ask her why she thought he was conceited.

"Because you've ignored me for two days," she said.
"Isn't Jack your date?"

"No, he's just a good friend. I hate blind dates, don't you?"

Bill laughed. "Most of the time I do," he said.

That began a nine-month courtship. They made plans to meet while Bill was at Fort Polk, Louisiana for two weeks of Army Reserve training. During those two weeks, they fell in love.

When Alice graduated from the University of Southwestern Louisiana, she took a teaching job in New Orleans. She and Bill took turns one weekend each month flying back and forth between New Orleans and Little Rock. Although Bill knew he was in love, getting married was a step he was reluctant to take until he got a nudge from Alice. She took the matter into her own hands and delivered an ultimatum in terms a Southerner understands. "Fish or cut bait."

Alice and Bill McArthur married February 1, 1964, at Golden Meadow, in Our Lady of Prompt Succor Catholic Church. Her wedding gown was the traditional white, and that was appropriate for her because she had saved herself for this day for twenty-two years. She wasn't naive about sex; however, her religion and her mother's advice always managed to override her passion, a fact Bill had accepted early in their relationship.

They were married in the afternoon and afterward Bill overheard his new brother-in-law joking, "That Cajun will tear that redneck up." Bill smiled to himself with the realization that even Alice's brother didn't really know her.

Alice had lived on the bayou all her life, and her wedding day must have represented not only the beginning of a new life as a wife, but the beginning of a whole new way of life. As Bill's convertible headed farther and farther away from her home, Alice must have felt a little as Bill did years earlier when he left Clinton.

Soon McArthur learned Alice's boisterous ways were just a front she put on when she was with their friends. Sometimes she was even a little vulgar because she enjoyed shocking her friends and making them laugh. But Alice was a different kind of person when she and McArthur were alone: quiet, subdued, and although she was skillful at making people think she was always in control, she really lacked self-confidence.

At first, Alice was unhappy in her new environment because she didn't have a job or friends and because Arkansas was like a foreign country, compared to the Cajun country of Louisiana. But by the time McArthur entered night law school that September, Alice had landed a teaching job at Joe T. Robinson Elementary School near Little Rock and was beginning to make some friends. After one year in public school, Alice started teaching at a Catholic elementary school.

For the next several years, McArthur and Alice grew accustomed to spending little time together. By the time McArthur finished law school in 1969, he was twenty-eight years old and had been so busy going to school and studying, he hadn't really noticed that he and Alice had grown apart. It only got worse when he started building his law practice. There was practically no time for the two of them.

McArthur's first job as a lawyer was working for another lawyer, Claude Carpenter, for $200 a week. His goal was to be the best trial lawyer in the state. He chose criminal law because that was where he thought he could get the most experience the fastest. It wasn't until later that the ramifications of this decision hit home: Because of McArthur's choice of profession, he became acquainted with more than his share of unsavory characters.

While working for Carpenter, McArthur met the circuit court judges, who appointed him to a lot of cases, and he gained valuable experience.

The first jury trial he handled was a first-degree murder case. Carpenter and another lawyer had been appointed to defend a black man named Clemmons Johnson, but they passed the case on to McArthur and another young lawyer, Fletcher Jackson. In a sink-or-swim situation, and with Johnson's permission, the two novice lawyers plunged headlong into their first major case.

Clemmons Johnson appeared to be a very gentle man, despite his large physical appearance. He had been a master sergeant in the Air Force. Once, while working as a bouncer at the Non-Commissioned Officers Club at the Little Rock Air Force Base, somebody had grabbed him from behind while he was breaking up a fight and choked him until he wet his pants.

Johnson went back to his quarters, changed, returned to the club, and killed the man who had choked him. He was discharged from the service after being court martialed and went to prison. After prison he came back home to Little Rock and his wife. Soon, however, he and his wife separated, and several weeks later, he found her in bed with another man. Johnson stabbed the man fifteen times with a kitchen knife, but the jury reduced the charge against Johnson from first-degree murder to manslaughter after listening to McArthur's closing argument.

McArthur had his first taste of victory. He knew victory for defense lawyers often meant something short of an outright acquittal. After the Johnson case, his reputation grew. He always went before a jury without a prepared text, but he didn't seem to need one. His ability to sway a jury favorably toward his clients and his skill as an orator won him more clients.

If he thought his client was guilty, McArthur never gave a clue, no matter how hard a juror searched his face. He became a master at concealing his true feelings from the jury, the judge and from others as well.

Bill and Alice's first child was planned to arrive after McArthur finished law school in 1969.

"I like Josh, Hank, Mark and Sean," Alice had said, looking up from the baby name book, hoping Bill would approve at least one of the names. She was already eight months pregnant, and they hadn't decided on a name.

"There are five thousand 'Seans' in the world," Bill said.

"Well, how about 'Bill, Jr.,'" she said.

"God, no! I don't want our son stuck with 'Junior' all his life. There's nothing worse than a grown man being called 'Junior.'"

It never occurred to either of them that their first child might not be a boy, and the only name they had picked by the time they arrived at the hospital was "Chuck."

Bill was seated in the fathers' waiting room of Saint Vincent Infirmary in Little Rock when the Sister told him about his new daughter. His surprise at having a girl was overtaken by amazement when he saw her the first time. He marveled at the perfection of her tiny shape and was awed by having taken part in the creation of a human life.

"By God, we did it," Alice beamed as Bill entered the recovery room. She was a little goofy from the anesthesia and the euphoria mothers often feel right after giving birth.

Bill leaned over and kissed her and told her how excited he was over their little daughter.

"What do you want to call her?" he asked.

"I don't know. I haven't thought about a girl's name."

"There's no rush," he said. "Are you all right?"

"By God, we did it!" Alice said again.

Bill laughed, "By God, we did!"

Two days later, Baby McArthur was named "Robyn."

Alice left teaching to devote herself full time to her new role of mother, and Bill continued to build his law practice diligently. Her friends said maybe she wasn't as happy with some of those early choices when she looked back on them later and regretted not having a career of her own. Alice gave freely and her children brought her the most satisfaction in life, but she began to feel that she had missed out on things she could have done well.

Two years after Robyn was born in 1973, Alice and Bill had their son.

"I had your boy!" Alice exclaimed when she first saw Bill after Chuck was born.

"I know you did, and I'm really proud of you," Bill said. "He's got to be the ugliest kid in the world."

"I believe you're right," Alice laughed.

But neither of them worried about their son's looks. They knew he wouldn't always be red and wrinkled.

It was some time after Chuck's arrival that McArthur's law practice began flourishing. He had gone into partnership with Floyd Lofton, a former law school classmate, and the two men worked well together and brought in substantial fees.

While McArthur was in partnership with Lofton, the McArthurs took their first and only real vacation—to the Bahamas. They were feeling good about Bill's career and for the first time in their marriage had no financial problems. They had realized their dream: Financial security, a new home, a family, a good career.

With his law practice secure by the late 1970s, McArthur found himself with time on his hands and money to spend. But he soon became bored. He was dissatisfied, restless. He felt life was passing him by.

That's when he met Ms. X.* Ms. X had long, dark hair and an oval face. Five-foot-three, she weighed about 130 pounds, but she didn't look pudgy. She was a nice-looking woman who dressed well. Ms. X had a moody personality, but that didn't matter; McArthur's attraction to her was not psychological, it was entirely physical. Ms. X, married to an older man, was bored with her life, too, and was equally attracted to McArthur. They managed to find places to meet. They used McArthur's secretary's apartment a couple of times and these meetings were always the same—sex was the primary objective. After that urge was satisfied, McArthur knew there wasn't anything else keeping the relationship alive, at least as far as he was concerned. So, after a few weeks, he tried to break off the affair. But Ms. X did not want to let him go. She was becoming more demanding, more possessive, more dangerous. She even began calling his house and hanging up when Alice answered the telephone and showing up at his office without warning. Once she followed him when he went to lunch. Another time she barged into his private office, closed the door and proceeded to take off her clothes.

"Get out," he said and threw her clothes at her.

"Okay, if that's the way you want it, I'll tell Alice everything."

"Then you'll just have to go ahead and tell her," he said, hoping she wouldn't.

She did, though, and not only did she tell Alice everything, she played tape recordings of her meetings with McArthur.

The tapes were her trump card, something she could use if McArthur got out of line. She simply called

---

*"Ms. X" is a fictitious name.

Alice one afternoon and played one of them over the telephone.

When McArthur got home from the office that afternoon, Alice confronted him, and all hell broke loose. He admitted the affair, begged forgiveness, swore he loved Alice and didn't care anything about the other woman. Alice insisted he take her to Ms. X's apartment so she could demand the tapes. She didn't want her family embarrassed by the tapes in spite of the anger and pain Bill had caused her. And perhaps she wanted to accomplish something else by going to see Ms. X. Perhaps she wanted the other woman to see that she and Bill stood united against her. Alice wanted the other woman to know she had lost, and Alice had won.

Ms. X let them inside, glaring at Alice haughtily. Bill's discomfort was obvious, but he said nothing. Alice did all the talking.

"I want those damn tapes, you bitch," Alice said.

"Well, you aren't going to get them."

"At least you could have picked somebody with a little class," Alice said to Bill, as she ground out her cigarette on Ms. X's kitchen floor.

Ms. X became furious. She slapped Alice, and before McArthur could stop them, the two women were down on the floor in a name-calling, hair-pulling, face-scratching fight.

A visitor, one of Ms. X's girlfriends, called the police when the fight broke out. Bill managed to pull Alice off Ms. X and get her out of the apartment before the police arrived, but Alice left without the tapes.

It was hard for Alice to accept what her husband had done. Fidelity was important to her, but her marriage was more important than her pride, so she accepted the situation. McArthur's conscience bothered him for a long time. He felt stupid for having risked his marriage and angry at himself for having hurt Alice's feelings so deeply.

I don't really have any knowledge of having ever gone through a midlife crisis. There were a lot of factors that contributed to it. From the time Alice and I got married ... I was working all day, going to school at night, fourteen–sixteen hour days. Then, when I started law practice, I had to keep just about the same hours trying to learn what to do because I was just thrown into a pile of cases and just had to make do. I had started building up a reputation as a lawyer, started making a little money. All those factors, I think, had something to do with this. Alice and I probably both got a little bored with each other, the things that usually happen in a marriage. To this day, I don't know how you can prevent that from happening. The one thing I guess you lose sight of is what's most important. You lose sight of what your priorities are, and I believe that's what I did.

... William C. "Bill" McArthur, 1984

Chapter Four

THE EVENTS THAT ERUPTED ONE INNOCENT March morning in 1981 changed Bill and Alice McArthur's lives forever. It started with a telephone call from Tom Glaze, a Court of Appeals judge. He told McArthur that a North Little Rock man named Ron Orsini had been found dead that morning, and the victim's wife, Lee Orsini, was someone the judge had become acquainted with as a result of the judge's work in the fathers' rights movement. Glaze asked McArthur to go to the North Little Rock Police Department to make sure Mrs. Orsini's rights were observed.

"Just check on things, Bill, and make sure things are going all right because as far as I know, no attorney has been called," Glaze said.

McArthur arrived at the police station before noon on March 12, 1981. Detective T.J. Farley and Officer Buddy Miles had already taken a statement from Mrs. Orsini by the time he arrived, and they let him read it prior to seeing her. They also had performed a trace metal test on her hands to determine if she had recently held a gun. Although the markings did not indicate she had held a gun, the test did register some marks on the fingertips of her right hand. Farley and Miles told McArthur that they had decided not to hold Orsini.

McArthur was then led into an interrogation room where Orsini had been questioned. A woman in her early 30s, she was wearing a big flannel shirt, possibly one of her husband's, McArthur thought, and dirty blue jeans, and her hair wasn't fixed up in any particular manner. She was visibly upset and crying, and when McArthur explained why he was there—to protect her rights—she started asking him why the police were holding her. She denied—without being asked by McArthur—any knowledge of what had happened to her husband, and she repeated what she had already told the police.

Orsini said her husband had dinner with her about 6:00 or 6:30 p.m. the previous evening. He retired for the evening to the master bedroom just before 10 p.m. She said she slept in her daughter's room—which was separated from the master bedroom by a closet and one wall—that night because the girl was ill, and neither she nor her daughter, Tiffany, heard any strange sounds during the night.

The next morning she and Tiffany noticed Ron's bedroom door was locked, but Orsini said she assumed it had accidentally locked, as it sometimes did, after her husband left for work. She decided to leave the door locked for the time being and take Tiffany to school. When she and Tiffany left the house, they noticed Ron's truck was still parked outside, but Orsini said she thought nothing unusual about that either. She said she thought perhaps the battery had died and Ron had ridden to work with one of his business partners.

On the way to Tiffany's junior high school, they made several stops: They ate breakfast at a restaurant, went to the grocery store and to a drugstore to look at some gold jewelry.

When they got to the school, Orsini took her daughter to the office and told the school secretary that Tiffany had not been feeling well and asked her to call her at home if Tiffany became ill at school. Before leaving, she also talked to the school nurse.

When she arrived at home, she decided to open her bedroom door by sticking an ice pick through the hole in the middle of the door knob—something she had done many times before, she said.

She couldn't see when she first entered the darkened room because heavy, custom-made draperies on the windows blocked out almost all of the sunlight, but as her senses adjusted to the pale quiet, she saw her husband's body lying face down on the bed. When she looked closer, she saw blood everywhere, and it looked like half of his face was missing.

As she told her story to McArthur, she wrung her hands and often stopped to sob into a tissue. She was pale and confused, McArthur thought, and he worried she might break down in her dazed state, so he offered to stay with her to help break the news to her daughter. McArthur and Orsini were standing outside the police station when the girl arrived and approached her mother.

"Something terrible has happened. Daddy's dead," Orsini said, holding her arms open to embrace the girl.

McArthur waited for the emotional reaction he was sure would follow—an initial shock, a burst of tears, then perhaps a collapse into her mother's waiting arms. But he was taken completely by surprise when the girl showed no reaction at all.

Ten days later Dr. Fahmy Malak, the state medical examiner, determined Ron Orsini, 38, was the victim of a homicide. He was killed by a .38-caliber bullet fired from a pistol that had been placed against the crown of his head, Malak said. The bullet exited through Ron's nose and was found on the bed near his body. Malak said Ron was most likely asleep at the time he was shot. Although Mrs. Orsini claimed Ron slept alone the night he was killed, police photographs indicate someone may have been in bed next to him because of indentations in the pillow and sheets.

Initially, Malak said he had not ruled out suicide.

One handgun was found in a chest of drawers in the bedroom, but it was later determined that neither that gun nor other guns found in the house were the murder weapon.

The police said the house showed no sign of forced entry, and Orsini said nothing had been stolen. They interviewed neighbors, but no one heard anything out of the ordinary except for one neighbor who said his dogs were upset during the evening and barked loudly. Both Tiffany and her mother claimed they did not hear a gunshot. The police searched creeks and drainage ditches near the Orsini home for the murder weapon, but none was found. Then they learned that in mid-January Ron Orsini had reported a Colt .38-caliber pistol—the same caliber and brand of gun believed to have been the murder weapon—was stolen from his truck.

About a week after the murder, while McArthur was trying a case in Pulaski County Circuit Court in Little Rock, he noticed Orsini sitting in the back of the courtroom. With her was a middle-aged man in glasses, who had brown curly hair and a receding hair line. The man had his arm around her.

When court adjourned, Orsini lagged behind the rest of the spectators and introduced McArthur to her companion, Dr. Charles H. Wulz, a Sherwood veterinarian.

Not long after their meeting in Circuit Court Orsini came to McArthur's office and retained him as her attorney and paid him $1,000. It was apparent by that time that the police considered her a suspect in her husband's death.

Four weeks after Orsini's death, the North Little Rock Police Department asked the Pulaski County Prosecuting Attorney, Wilbur C. "Dub" Bentley, to seek a grand jury investigation into Ron Orsini's death. About the same time, McArthur told prosecutor Bentley such an investigation would be welcome because it would prove his client was not involved in her husband's death. Also in April, Orsini was appointed executrix of her husband's will. That move prompted Ron Orsini's former wife to contest the appointment on behalf of his daughter from that marriage, Stacy Renee Orsini, nine, who was living in Shreveport, Louisiana. In a probate hearing in late May, attorneys for the child referred to Orsini as a "prime suspect" in her husband's death.

During the three months following Ron Orsini's death, Lee Orsini continuously expressed to the news media her dissatisfaction with the investigative efforts of the North Little Rock Police Department and hired a private investigator to look into the case. At the same time, she began lengthy conversations with McArthur in preparation for the inevitable grand jury. She said large sums of money had appeared in their house several times. She had become concerned because Ron seemed upset, withdrawn, nervous, even scared. On one occasion, she had followed Ron and witnessed a meeting between him and some men in a plain car, perhaps an unmarked police car. She told McArthur she thought her husband had gotten involved in something illegal, possibly drugs, and since his death, she had been receiving strange phone calls. On several occasions the caller had threatened her.

In early June, Lee Orsini was again in the news. She told police she surprised a man early one morning in her home on Pontiac Drive as he was removing bags containing an unknown white substance from a secret compartment in the bottom of a bookshelf in her den. She said she held a gun on the man while she reached for a telephone to call the police, but he lunged at her, tearing her nightgown; and, in a struggle over the gun, the gun discharged. She said she might have injured the man because he screamed and fled.

McArthur began preparing a defense for Orsini.

One of the first things he did was hire a private investigator, Jim Lester, a former Arkansas State Police investigator on medical leave from the State Police at the time of the Orsini homicide. Lester's job was to make a security check of the Orsini home on Pontiac Drive to establish any evidence of a break-in, interview neighbors and gather evidence that would support Orsini's innocence. As part of his job, Lester interviewed Orsini on several occasions, attempting to form his own opinion regarding her guilt or innocence. Regardless of what he finally decided, however, he was committed to her defense, and would do everything he could to help build that defense.

Lester was a rough-edged cop with graying hair, a gravel voice and the build of a professional wrestler. He was known as a superb investigator responsible for several murder convictions. His methods were unconventional but shrewd. He did anything he felt necessary to gain a suspect's trust and confidence, even if it meant he had to play the role of father confessor or big brother to coax a confession out of someone. Once Lester even got a confession from a murder suspect by getting down on his knees in the cell and praying with him. Lester enjoyed his role-playing and was good at it, for outwardly he seemed sincere, and the flood of emotion he was able to turn off and on so overwhelmed his suspects they soon regarded him as their best friend and would share their innermost thoughts with him. With a belief in the basic evil of man and the skepticism and bitterness that came from years of working in law enforcement, Lester accepted the Orsini assignment from McArthur.

In some ways, Lester's job of preparing a defense for Orsini was made easier by the North Little Rock Police Department. When they first arrived at the Orsini home, they assumed Ron had committed suicide, and, consequently, were not as careful about preserving the crime scene as they might have been. After the coroner checked the body and it was removed to the medical examiner's laboratory for an autopsy, the police allowed Ron's business partners to take all the bedding—including the mattress and box springs—and burn it.

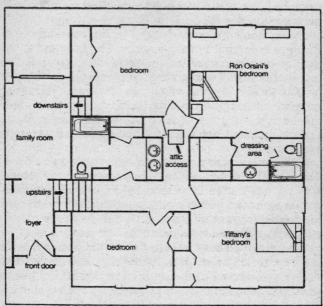

Floor plans of the bedrooms in the Orsini home.

ing, Lester met with McArthur to discuss Lester's progress on the Orsini case:

"I know she's guilty," the private investigator said, propping his feet up on the lawyer's desk and taking a deep draw of his cigarette, letting the smoke curl around his lips. He looked McArthur directly in the eyes, waiting for what he said to sink in.

"Fine, where's the evidence? Where's the gun?" McArthur countered in his best defense lawyer demeanor. "Where's the towel with the gunpowder marks on it? All the other things you have to have to prove this, where are they?"

"There was a towel in the wash that had holes and stuff in it . . ."

"Come to my house someday, Jim, and you'll find some of these at my house. They're used for dust rags, car washing, and we do wash them."

"Now, don't get me wrong. I'm on your side. I'm going to help you, but she's guilty. The little girl's bed is only ten feet away, as the crow flies, from Ron's bed—only a wall and a closet separate them. There's no way on God's green earth you can fire a .38-caliber weapon and anyone in that 2,300-square-foot house not hear it, unless you're comatose," Lester said. "I know damn well Lee's guilty—she's a devious, treacherous woman."

"Oh, Jim, you're just a damn old cop, and you think like one. Prove she's guilty." He came out from behind his desk and patted Lester's shoulder as the older man got up to leave. Lester again looked at McArthur and felt a need to warn him.

"Look, Bill, that woman is evil," he said.

"She may be guilty as hell, I don't know, but I don't see any proof of it, Jim. Sure, she admittedly was sleeping in a room in the upstairs section of the house when the man was shot, but that doesn't prove she did it."

Realizing the importance of a convincing polygraph test, Lester and McArthur scheduled one for Orsini, but she flunked it, so they arranged for another one. She flunked it again. Lester then suggested he and Orsini travel to Chicago to see J.E. Reid, a renowned polygraphist used by the famous criminal defense attorney, F. Lee Bailey. Orsini refused. Later, she arranged for her own polygraph, which she passed.

Meanwhile, Lester went through Lee Orsini's house carefully, checking for any evidence of a forced entry or anything a good defense attorney could use to convince a jury one was attempted. But instead of finding such evidence, he found what appeared to his trained eye to be a novice's attempt at staging a forced entry. Nevertheless, Lester found a locksmith who would be willing to testify someone could enter a home without it appearing it had been broken into.

His other investigations uncovered the Orsinis' strained finances and Lee Orsini's propensity to spend much more than the meager income her husband earned from his air conditioning business. At the time of Ron Orsini's death, Lee Orsini was unemployed and bills were stacked up. Yet, Ron had just purchased a $2,600 boat and motor which he planned to use for a fishing trip the next weekend.

Lester also learned a lot about Ron Orsini. He talked to many people who had known Orsini, and they all agreed he was a good man, a family man, a hard worker, a blue-collar worker with conservative, traditional values. He certainly was not the type of man who would become involved in drug deals.

During his weeks of investigations, Lester made several attempts at interviewing Tiffany, but each time he mentioned it to Orsini, she either changed the subject or made an excuse for Tiffany not to be interviewed. She told Lester the girl could not be questioned regarding the tragic loss of her stepfather. She told Lester perhaps he could talk to Tiffany later, after she had sufficient time to adjust.

In interviewing Orsini, Lester tried the tactics he learned from his years of criminal investigation. He always tried to get the truth out of his subject first—whether that truth meant the subject was guilty or innocent—then work on a defense or prosecution. Late one afternoon while interviewing Orsini in McArthur's office after the lawyer had left for the day, Lester felt he touched something within her conscience when he tried to let her justify the murder to him:

"You know, Lee, there are many reasons why one might be justified in killing someone—maybe not 'justified,' but there are reasons. Maybe he beat you, Lee. Was he doing something to your daughter and you found out about it . . . ?"

During this line of questioning, she began to weep, and she turned to Lester, saying in a voice that was almost a whisper, "Oh, Jim, if I could only tell you."

Meanwhile, Orsini was enjoying her new celebrity status with the local press. Each new development—such as the threatening phone calls and finding the burglar in her den—somehow leaked out to one or both of the two statewide newspapers or to one of the three network-affiliated television stations. Orsini was particularly vocal in her criticism of how the North Little Rock Police handled the investigation. On several occasions McArthur chastised his client for making statements to the press. Each time she would tell him that the reporters called her first and that she really didn't tell them anything at all: "They built this whole story around a couple of answers I gave them to some little insignificant questions. Really, Bill, I didn't say anything. I can't imagine where they're getting their information from."

On July 8, 1981 a Pulaski County grand jury began investigating the Ron Orsini homicide. Less than a month later, after interviewing forty-seven witnesses, it returned "no true bill," which meant there would be no indictment.

Orsini, however, remained one of McArthur's clients after the grand jury. He handled several civil matters for her as a result of her husband's death and her deteriorating financial situation. She called McArthur's secretary, Phoebe Jones, practically every day. The two women were fast becoming friends. And the rest of the summer was quiet. That is, except for one afternoon when Orsini called her lawyer, saying she needed to talk to him right away about something important. She wouldn't say what it was over the phone, but she insisted it was urgent and that she speak to him in person immediately and away from his office because she might be followed. McArthur related this to Lester the next day:

"Yesterday I got a call from Orsini. She said there was some big thing going on, and she had to meet me right away. She told me to meet her at Murray Lock and Dam. When I got there, she had sandwiches and wine!" McArthur exclaimed, noting a sudden change in Lester's countenance.

"Bill, leave that bitch alone. She's crazy," Lester said.

"You know, Jim, it really shocked me when I got down there—there was no trauma—no biggy—I got down there, and she had sandwiches and wine!" McArthur exclaimed.

"Stay away for her. She'll put you in a trick bag," Lester said.

"Ain't no way I'd have anything to do with that woman," McArthur said.

She did not like him at all. She never did, and a great deal of it was because of his perceptiveness. She was always talking about how much she disliked Jim Lester.

. . . William C. "Bill" McArthur, 1984

Chapter Five

PHOEBE JONES WAS THE YOUNGEST OF three children. Her parents owned a small motel and restaurant in Ozark, Arkansas, a tiny town in the northwest part of the state. Ozark is the kind of community where everybody knows everybody else's business, where teen-agers drive their cars around town at night and sit in the parking lots downtown because that's all there is to do. Phoebe used to join her friends on Friday and Saturday nights, sitting on the hoods of their cars, most of which were pickup trucks, but Phoebe refused to ride in those trucks because she was a little stuck-up. She thought pickup trucks were crude and boys who drove them, boorish. Whenever Phoebe's mother caught her participating in the parking lot ritual, she got in trouble because her mother said it wasn't "ladylike."

Phoebe played the tenor saxophone in the high school band, and like many other kids from small towns, Phoebe had a lot of pets. Her favorite was a rooster named Pinky. Phoebe, a dark-haired girl with gray eyes, had natural beauty which makeup enhanced. Later in life she had a problem with her weight and spent a lot of time, energy and money going on fad diets or joining health spas, but while she was in high school, she had a well-proportioned figure and often entered beauty contests. That's where she got the idea she would grow up to be a dental hygienist—because it sounded like something good to tell beauty contest judges.

Upon graduation from high school in 1970, Phoebe spent what she later called the "two worst years of my entire life" attending Arkansas Tech University in Russellville, another small town about an hour's drive from Ozark. When her father realized he was wasting his money sending his daughter to college, he allowed her to drop out and take an accounting course offered by a vocational school. She was still a long way from becoming a dental hygienist when she left Ozark in June 1973 in a green Maverick she had learned to drive only a month before. Her destination was Texas. She had always wanted to get out of Ozark and live on her own, and moving to Texas wouldn't be as frightening as moving to New York or California. After all, she had an aunt in San Antonio.

But before she could cross the state line, Phoebe decided she needed time to gain a little experience in the job market, and at the same time, earn some money to stake her move to Texas. So she took a job in Little Rock with a company that sold electrical and plumbing supplies. At least Little Rock was far enough away from Ozark that people wouldn't be reporting her every move to her parents. That was the thing she hated the most about a small town—people nosing around in her business.

After working at the electrical and plumbing supply company for a little more than a year, Phoebe went to an employment agency and found out about a legal secretarial job in the McArthur and Lassiter law firm in Little Rock. In 1974 she took the job because it paid $425 a month, an increase over her other job.

McArthur, whose law practice was thriving, had gone into practice with Jack Lassiter and now needed more help. He was getting big criminal cases and large fees, and Phoebe knew that the work would be exciting, especially for a twenty-one-year-old girl from a small town. Phoebe took pride in her work and wanted to learn as much as she could, and McArthur gave her the opportunity. It didn't take long for her to become more of an assistant to him than a secretary. She was sharp and eager. McArthur knew her small-town background and felt a little protective of her. Over the years, he became more of a big brother to her than a boss. Whenever she had a problem, she knew she could turn to her boss for help. He loaned her money, counseled her on her love life, and advised her whenever he thought she needed it. They became friends, not in any romantic way, but in a relationship of mutual trust.

Phoebe liked the new offices the McArthur and Lassiter firm moved into in March 1981, an English tudor home converted into offices. The large, old house was about a mile from downtown, and the distance from the courthouse was the only drawback to the new location, but Phoebe thought the extra room the new offices afforded would make up for the inconvenience of having to drive downtown every time she needed to file papers for her boss. She liked having her own office, just across the foyer from the receptionist, but she hated answering the telephone, so she convinced McArthur to hire her niece, Diane Dutton, to handle that responsibility.

Phoebe met Lee Orsini for the first time just a week or so before the firm moved to its new location. During the grand jury investigation into Ron Orsini's death, Phoebe only talked to Mrs. Orsini for the purpose of making appointments for her with McArthur and for other business matters.

The day the grand jury returned "no true bill," Bill McArthur attended a champagne party at Orsini's home. When he arrived, he was shocked to find both Dr. Wulz and the press on hand. The next day Orsini called Phoebe and said, "Bill's really mad at me."

"Lee, I've heard about the champagne party, and it's

not good to have you and Dr. Wulz on the front page of the paper. He does have a past, you know."

"Oh, Phoebe, we're just good friends."

"That may be, but like Bill told you, do you want to smear this in the public's face? It was wrong, Lee."

"I know. I know. I know."

"It looks bad," Phoebe said.

Charles Wulz practiced veterinary medicine in Duncan, Oklahoma, from 1956 until 1974. On March 18, 1969, he awakened at 6:30 a.m. to find his twenty-nine-year-old wife, Ann, dead beside him in bed. He was charged with her murder after the Oklahoma medical examiner's autopsy report stated the cause of death was "smothering—homicide." Wulz spent seven months in jail awaiting trial. The trial lasted from October 20 to November 2, 1969, but the jury became deadlocked after twenty-six hours of deliberation and a mistrial was declared. He was released on bond and stood trial a second time from April 1 to April 17, 1970. This time he was acquitted.

The state medical examiner said at Wulz's trial that Mrs. Wulz's death was intentional smothering. The only way "a symmetrical injury could be inflicted on the back of the airway is pressure from the front." A toxicologist testified her lungs were not found to be congested; therefore, her death was sudden. But the defense argued Mrs. Wulz had taken too many sleeping pills, rolled over onto her pillow and suffocated. The toxicologist agreed with the defense that ". . . anything is possible."

"She could have rolled over," the toxicologist said, but he also said he did not agree with that theory.

The state also brought out evidence Mrs. Wulz had decided to leave Wulz for another man and take their eighteen-month-old daughter, Tammy, with her. In fact, Mrs. Wulz's father testified that right after his daughter's death, Wulz told him, "I am a misfit. Ann was trying to get away, and if I had let her go, she would be here today."

The defense called five medical experts to back their contention that Mrs. Wulz either died of an overdose of drugs or accidentally suffocated while in a drug-induced coma. One of those experts, Dr. George Murphy, a psychiatry professor from Washington University in St. Louis, Missouri, testified he believed Ann Wulz committed suicide by taking an overdose of phenobarbitol. Dr. Henry Siegel, the chief medical examiner of Westchester County, New York, said bruises found on the back of the airway and along the flarings of the nose were hemorrhages that could have occurred either before or after death. He said if they occurred after death—which he said was most likely—they could have been caused by several things, including a post-mortem body reaction.

Wulz took the stand himself and testified the marriage was a "tug-of-war" with him on one side trying to preserve it and his wife's mother and sister on the other side trying to break it up. But he said on the night of March 17, 1969, the night before his wife died, she told him things she had never talked about before —she talked of her family life, her parents and events dating back to childhood—and at the end of that conversation, he felt she intended to stay with him instead of filing for divorce.

After seven hours of closing statements by the defense and prosecution, a "not guilty" verdict was returned.

Wulz stayed in Duncan, practicing veterinary medicine and living a quiet, uneventful life. He already had been divorced once and widowed once, and although he wasn't eager to jump into another marriage, about a year after his acquittal, he began dating a recently divorced woman named Claudia who had just moved to Duncan with her young son.

Wulz was open with her regarding his past. He often talked about the two trials and went into detail about the case. Sometimes he would become angry when talking about the police and the prosecutors and tell her how foolish they all were and how someday he hoped to pay them back for what they had done to him. Wulz and the woman married. They adopted each other's children and in 1974, they moved to Sherwood, Arkansas, near North Little Rock, where Wulz purchased a veterinary clinic, hoping to spare his daughter the pain of his past—a past he knew would always be remembered by Duncan gossips.

In 1976 Charles and Claudia Wulz divorced. She eventually remarried and moved to another small town near Little Rock. Wulz remained in Sherwood and maintained his veterinary practice. Several years later, his daughter enrolled in a dancing class, where she met new friends. One of them was Tiffany Orsini.

This lady called me one day and was questioning me about Charles—what kind of man he was. She said she was in love with him and wanted to find out if these things about him were true because she thought he was about to ask her to marry him. I said, 'If there's anything you want to know about Dr. Wulz, I suggest you call and ask him.' She asked me if I thought he killed his wife and asked why we broke up. I didn't think it was any of her business. I know it was Lee.

. . .Claudia, Dr. Charles Wulz's former wife, 1984

I dated Lee Orsini. I dated Lee Orsini because I got involved in this, not because I was attracted to Lee Orsini. . . . she knows that. . . . I was involved with her because of this situation, not because I was in love with her.

. . . Dr. Charles Wulz, 1984

Chapter Six

REPORTERS LOVE TO COVER TOMMY F. ROB-
inson. They get a vicarious thrill when they get near
his type—a reckless talker and tough, hard-nosed
crime fighter. But looking back on his career, it might
be said his reputation was merely an image created by
the Arkansas news media.

Robinson already had spent many years in law enforcement by the time he was elected sheriff of Pulaski
County, Arkansas, in 1980. After graduating from
North Little Rock High School in 1959, Robinson had
joined the Navy, where he decided to enter law enforcement. He got his first criminal justice job in 1963
as a patrolman for the North Little Rock Police Department. He stayed there until May 1966, when he
became a trooper for the Arkansas State Police. In
1968 he left the state police and went back to the
North Little Rock Police Department until 1971, when
he became a member of the United States Marshal's
Service for the Eastern District of Arkansas. He left
the Marshal's Service in 1974 to take a job as the assistant director of public safety at the University of Arkansas in Fayetteville. A short time later he was
transfered to Little Rock as director of public safety at
the University of Arkansas medical science campus
until August 1975.

Robinson first gained media attention in 1975 when
he was named police chief of Jacksonville, Arkansas, a

city with a population of about 20,000 at that time, located a few miles north of Little Rock and encompassing the Little Rock Air Force Base. One of the first things he did was tell the local Rotary Club that Jacksonville had a drug problem and an unprofessional police force. Then he instituted strict policies, cracking down on back-room gambling. He also fired several city policemen, some of whom took their cases before the city's Civil Service Commission.

By the time Robinson had been in office at Jacksonville six months, he had come under criticism from members of the Civil Service Commission, had $350,000 in lawsuits filed against him and the city, and been accused of using the Jacksonville Police Department for politically motivated investigations.

While he was police chief of Jacksonville, Robinson met Bill McArthur, who represented several of the police officers who had been fired by Robinson. McArthur got them reinstated, and after Robinson had been police chief for two years, McArthur was appointed special judge in a contempt-of-court case against Robinson.

The contempt charge resulted from a feud Robinson had with Jacksonville Municipal Judge Reed Williamson. About a year after taking the job as Jacksonville police chief, Robinson told a criminal justice class at the University of Arkansas at Little Rock that Judge Williamson was "a real bastard." A student journalist listening to Robinson's lecture reported his remark in the school newspaper, and Judge Williamson initiated contempt proceedings against the police chief.

McArthur's order in the contempt case stated he would dismiss the charge against Robinson if the chief would apologize publicly as well as deliver a written apology to the judge. Robinson complied with McArthur's decision, but he wasn't happy about it. He would long remember Bill McArthur's decision.

* * *

John Shepherd became a member of the Jacksonville
Police Department after retiring in 1974 from the Air
Force. He had been stationed at the Little Rock Air
Force Base and was town liaison officer for the base.
During that time, he knew the police officers at Jacksonville well, and when he left the Air Force, they en-
couraged him to join their ranks. He did so shortly
before Robinson became police chief. One of the officers Shepherd met when he joined the department
was Bobby Woodward.

Woodward had a penchant for firearms. Co-workers
who thought Woodward was obsessed with weapons
had seen him "playing" with guns and even shooting
holes into the floor of a trailer behind the police station that housed the Criminal Investigation Division.
One quiet Sunday afternoon before Robinson became
chief, John Shepherd was on radio duty at the Jacksonville Police Department when he noticed Woodward and another officer enter the station for a coffee
break. Shepherd was in the radio room, separated
from the coffee area by a glass partition. While he
looked on, he saw Woodward and the other patrolman
take their service revolvers out of their holsters and
begin to pretend they were shooting each other. They
twirled the weapons around like children playing cowboys, laughed and ducked the make-believe blasts they
aimed at each other.

Woodward soon left the department but asked to be
rehired after Robinson became chief. When Robinson
was considering Woodward's application to rejoin the
Jacksonville Police Department, he called Shepherd
and a couple of other officers into his office and asked
them if they thought he should rehire Woodward.

"No. From what I have seen, Bobby Woodward is
an immature individual," Shepherd replied, and the
other officers agreed that under no circumstances
should Robinson rehire him. A few days later Wood-

ward was hired and made a member of the Criminal
Investigation Division, a new department created by
Robinson.

Sometime in late 1977, a Jacksonville police officer
heard about McArthur's affair with Ms. X. The officer
was a good friend of one of Ms. X's girlfriends. When
discussing McArthur's stint as special judge, the
woman laughingly told the officer about the affair
McArthur was having with her friend, thinking it was
humorous to imagine McArthur in a judge's robe one
minute and in a compromising position another. She
joked about the irony and even mentioned the fact Ms.
X had, without McArthur's knowledge, tape-recorded
several of their rendezvous so she could listen to them
whenever she was unable to be with McArthur.

Not long after Ms. X's girlfriend made these revela-
tions to the Jacksonville police officer, the officer offered her $300 if she could get one of these tapes, and
he didn't care how she got it. She asked him why he
would need such a tape, and he replied: "We just want
something to hang over his head," he said. When she
refused to steal her friend's tapes, the officer upped
the ante to $600, but she remained adamant.

About this time, Jim Lewis, a young patrolman at
Jacksonville, walked into Robinson's office one afternoon and heard Robinson and two of his officers listening to a tape-recording on Robinson's desk and
laughing. The voices on the tape were those of a man
and woman. He later realized the male voice on the
tape belonged to Bill McArthur.

Lewis became increasingly uneasy as he witnessed
some of the things going on at the Jacksonville Police
Department under Robinson. He hadn't heard the entire tape, but he could tell what the substance of it
was, and he suspected similar things were going on
within the department. His suspicions were confirmed
one day when he witnessed an injustice being done to

a fellow officer who had been fired by Robinson but reinstated after he hired Bill McArthur to represent him at a hearing before the Jacksonville Civil Service Commission.

One of Robinson's CID investigators at Jacksonville found out that the officer, who was married, was having an affair. The investigator developed times and dates indicating when the officer was with his girlfriend, and Robinson asked Lewis to write an anonymous letter to the officer's wife about the matter. When Lewis refused, Robinson became angry, but when Lewis threatened to go to the Civil Service Commission with a complaint, Robinson quickly cooled down.

Lewis, who was then a sergeant, was involved in the surveillance—by Jacksonville policemen—of the campaign headquarters of John Hardin, who was running for mayor. Robinson supported Hardin's opponent, and he told Lewis and several other officers to place special infrared equipment on a rooftop near the Hardin campaign headquarters to identify police officers and other people going in and out of the campaign headquarters.

One of the men seen entering the headquarters was Officer John Shepherd. A few days later a captain at the Jacksonville Police Department showed Lewis a bug he had placed on Shepherd's office telephone. The captain was proud of this device, and bragged to Lewis that "we" want to make sure Shepherd isn't leaking information outside the department. Later, after becoming disenchanted with Robinson, Lewis went to Shepherd and told him about the bug.

In addition to forming a Criminal Investigation Division, another of Robinson's initiatives while at Jacksonville was to organize a Special Weapons and Tactics team. The SWAT team was equipped with automatic weapons.

After Robinson left the Jacksonville Police Department and Shepherd became police chief, Shepherd was approached by a federal Alcohol, Tobacco and Firearms agent who asked about a machine gun which was registered to the Jacksonville Police Department but could not be located.

Shepherd asked his officers if they knew anything about the gun, and one of them told him a local physician had it. Shepherd sent an officer to the doctor's office to retrieve the gun. When the officer returned with it, he told Shepherd the doctor was surprised when he learned he was in possession of the gun illegally. Shepherd was surprised, though, when he learned the doctor had paid money for the gun.

Robinson created controversy and made headlines no matter where he went. Governor Bill Clinton appointed him director of the state Department of Public Safety in January 1979, and he feuded with the director of the state police and on several occasions leaked negative rumors to the news media about the state police. The head of the state police wasn't alone. Robinson also vilified the news media in general. He once called reporters "pimps" for judges and later referred to a state senator and two other sheriffs as "pimps." All of these individuals had in some way criticized Robinson or opposed him on an issue.

The situation was the same when Robinson was elected sheriff of Pulaski County, where Little Rock is located, in November 1980. Some black residents of the county accused his deputies of brutality not long after he took office in January 1981. He later made headlines for chaining prisoners to the fence of the state Department of Correction facilities after the state refused to accept them. He also made headlines when:

He pulled a gun on a young man who made an obscene gesture at him; he suggested putting up a bounty to send someone to the Soviet Union to bring back the person responsible for shooting down a Korean airliner; he arrested the county judge and county comptroller for refusing to approve certain payments to the sheriff's department, and they subsequently sued him for $4.5 million for false arrest; and he called George Howard, a black federal judge, a "token judge" and said he would not coddle prisoners with "fried chicken and watermelon," implying the judge would. Due to problems at the county jail, Judge Howard appointed a special jail master to oversee jail operations, but Robinson verbally abused the federal jail master and ordered him to leave the jail. The judge found Robinson in contempt of court for these actions and ordered Robinson jailed at a federal facility at Memphis, Tennessee. Robinson spent two nights in jail before returning to Little Rock, where he received a hero's welcome for his defiance of the federal judge.

Throughout his law enforcement career, Robinson took care of his friend Bobby Woodward. As head of the state Department of Public Safety, Robinson was in a position to get Woodward a job as an agent for the state Alcohol Beverage Control Board. And still later, when Robinson left his job with the state to become the Pulaski County sheriff, he brought Woodward with him and made him a captain in the Sheriff's Department.

When they were in Jacksonville, Robinson and Woodward were like loose cannons on deck, as far as Bill McArthur was concerned, and they both would reappear in McArthur's life at a time when he was powerless to alter the course of events they set in motion.

*   *   *

He [Robinson] uses things he knows about people. Everybody has a skeleton in their closet, and he uses it for his benefit.

...John Shepherd, 1985
Former Jacksonville Police Chief

Chapter Seven

AFTER THE GRAND JURY INVESTIGATION
into Ron Orsini's death, McArthur handled several
civil matters for Lee Orsini. She was often sued by
creditors, and the paperwork on her cases alone kept
McArthur's secretary, Phoebe, much busier than she
liked to be. It was during this time McArthur began
making plans to open a country-western nightclub.

Phoebe and Lee discussed the plans for the club on
the telephone many times. They even planned what
they would wear opening night: tight, shiny jeans and
cowboy boots.

Lee told Phoebe she had talked to McArthur about
the possibility of getting a loan on her Pontiac Drive
home and investing in the club, but when McArthur
got the financing from someone else, Lee told Phoebe
it didn't bother her. In fact, she said she was unable to
get a loan on her home anyway.

Phoebe's and Lee's friendship was distant until after
McArthur's club, BJ's Star Studded Honky Tonk,
opened in December 1981. During late 1981 and early
1982, Lee began calling Phoebe at least once a day,
sometimes more, most of the time just to talk about
matters unrelated to Orsini's legal problems. They
talked about Phoebe's recent marriage, about the club,
about Tiffany. On several of these occasions Lee mentioned to Phoebe she and Dr. Wulz were going to the
theater together that evening, or out to dinner. She
often indicated to Phoebe she had been in contact with

McArthur about personal matters. For instance, if they were discussing the club, Lee would say, "Oh, Bill and I talked about that the other day." Phoebe did not doubt Orsini had been in contact with McArthur, and she never questioned Orsini's statements. Orsini's and Phoebe's conversations consisted of small talk, and some of that small talk concerned Bill and Alice McArthur.

When McArthur opened BJ's Star Studded Honky Tonk in December 1981, it became an overnight success. Its major competitor, Kountry Klub Kowboy Disco, owned by Bob Troutt, stood practically empty while hundreds of country-western music fans flocked to BJ's to hear live entertainment from Nashville. The McArthurs and James Nelson, who was in the insurance business, each owned forty percent of the club. Another drawing card for BJ's was Bob Robbins, who worked at KSSN-FM, the most popular country radio station in Little Rock. Robbins, whose real name was Robert Spears, had worked at Troutt's club, but McArthur and Nelson gave Robbins a twenty percent interest in BJ's to leave Troutt's club and become the disc jockey at BJ's.

Not long after BJ's opened, Troutt filed a $1.7 million copyright suit against the owners of BJ's, claiming they had pirated the idea of a country-western disco from him. Then, on January 15, someone tried to torch BJ's, but the fire was minor and no one was injured.

In January or February 1982, Lee told Phoebe she was taking a trip to Colorado. Phoebe suspected she would be going with Wulz because Lee had said she was dating him. When Lee returned, Phoebe noticed strange things started happening. Lee said she was getting threatening phone calls, hang-up phone calls, calls from people who seemed to know something about

Ron's death. McArthur advised her to have the telephone company put a call-tracing device on her phone.

On March 11 Orsini observed the anniversary of her husband's death by placing flowers on his grave and announcing to the news media she was conducting her own investigation of his death.

Sheriff Robinson was in the news often in March. He announced to the media he was investigating Bob Troutt, the owner of the nightclub in competition with McArthur's club, for alleged criminal activity. On April 7 disc jockey Bob Robbins was severely beaten in the face with a baseball bat as he left the radio station where he worked. He was hospitalized and had to undergo reconstructive facial surgery. The next day Orsini showed up at Phoebe's office, breathless, frightened, shaking and almost unable to talk: "Someone tried to kill me." She was hysterical. She told Phoebe and McArthur someone had just shot at her while she was driving near the North Little Rock Airport. Phoebe fixed Orsini a Scotch and water to calm her down, and Phoebe and McArthur went outside to look at Orsini's car and saw that a bullet had shattered the driver's-side window. The next day Orsini announced to the news media she was abandoning her investigation into her husband's death, "because I'm not going to get killed over it."

A few days later, Robinson announced he would investigate the Ron Orsini murder. On April 13 Robinson arrested Troutt and charged him with arranging Robbins's beating. In late April the Troutt investigation took Robinson and his chief investigator, Major Larry Dill, to Honduras, where Troutt supposedly had an interest in a lobster farm. Upon his return from Honduras, Robinson arrested Troutt a second time and charged him with solicitation to murder two Honduran businessmen. As a result of that arrest, Troutt brought brutality charges against Robinson, but the Justice Department declined to prosecute the charges.

Troutt had operated nightclubs in Little Rock for 11 years before closing his country disco shortly after his first arrest. Before entering the nightclub business, Troutt was an aide to former Governor Orval Faubus. Prior to serving as a gubernatorial aide, Troutt was a reporter for the *Arkansas Democrat*. He won a libel lawsuit in 1959 against a competing newspaper, the *Arkansas Gazette*, after it printed allegations that he had taken a bribe in return for not writing exposes about gambling law violations.

Sheriff Robinson eventually filed 12 felony charges against Troutt, including contract arsons and beatings, but all the charges were subsequently dropped except the one for the Robbins beating.

In the meantime, both McArthur and Phoebe thought the North Little Rock Police Department was not doing as much as it should in the investigation of the thirteen-month-old Orsini homicide, and they sincerely feared for Lee Orsini's life.

"One of these days, we're going to get a phone call, and someone's going to tell us Lee's dead, and no one is doing anything about it," Phoebe said to McArthur the day Orsini's car was shot at, and he agreed with her.

Phoebe drafted a mortgage to McArthur from Orsini on April 2 on the home she owned on Shoshoni—Mrs. Hatcher's residence—for $25,000. Since Metropolitan Bank held a $30,000 mortgage on the same piece of property, McArthur's was a second mortgage. Because Orsini had only paid McArthur $1,000 toward his attorney's fees and had no cash, she offered the mortgage as payment of all attorney's fees that had accrued or would accrue as a result of the civil work McArthur was doing for her. McArthur, who did not know this was Mrs. Hatcher's home, thought Orsini would eventually sell the home so he could be paid for his work. He and Orsini agreed that if his final fee was less than the amount of the mortgage, he would return any unused portion of the $25,000 to her.

During the last two weeks of April, Phoebe mentioned to Orsini that McArthur's forty-fourth birthday was May 3. The two women planned a surprise birthday party for him, to be held at the office.

Orsini agreed to get the cake and champagne for the party as well as a gift for McArthur, a new briefcase, and Phoebe said she would reimburse her for half the expenses. Phoebe told McArthur's law partner about the party, and everyone kept the secret until 4 p.m. Only the office personnel and Orsini attended the surprise party. Alice was never invited to office parties.

Phoebe had married a few months earlier and in May, 1982, her husband, Paul Pinkston, opened a pawn shop in North Little Rock. Phoebe started spending a lot of time there before and after work and on Saturdays, and Orsini soon began dropping by the pawn shop to visit Phoebe. She even took some items there for Phoebe's husband to sell for her.

On Friday, May 21, 1982, Phoebe was still at the pawn shop when a call came from Orsini about 9 a.m. She told Phoebe she had just been on the telephone with Bill, who was at his office, and right in the middle of their conversation, Alice called him on another line: "He had to leave and go home. Alice's car was blown up or something," Orsini said. "I can't make head nor tail of what's going on."

"What! I'll just call out there and find out," Phoebe exclaimed. She put Orsini on hold and called the McArthur house on the other line. Alice answered the phone.

"Hell, I guess you're all right, I'm talking to you. Are you all right?" Phoebe asked.

"Yes. Bill's on his way out here."

Phoebe told Orsini that Alice wasn't hurt, except for a few scratches. Orsini and Phoebe stayed in telephone contact with each other all day, talking about any new shred of information they could get about what had happened and speculating about who was behind it. They agreed that the car bomb probably had something to do with the McArthurs' club, and they wondered if Bob Troutt was involved.

Sometime in May Orsini came by the office to see Phoebe about a new method of weight control. Phoebe was always complaining to Lee about being overweight.

"You're going to think I'm crazy. You can't ask me anything about it, but it works," Orsini said, smiling mischievously.

"Okay, I'm ready to try anything," Phoebe said.

"I need a lock of your hair," Orsini said.

"You are crazy!"

"No, now listen—it really works."

So, Phoebe took the scissors out of her desk drawer and clipped a lock of her hair and gave it to Orsini.

"This better work, Lee," Phoebe said doubtfully.

Two weeks later Orsini asked Phoebe if she had lost any weight.

"I'm not doing anything but gaining weight, Lee. What have you done to me?"

The two women laughed about Phoebe's problem, and Phoebe didn't think about it any more until Orsini brought it up over the telephone a few days later. Phoebe had mentioned that McArthur was trying to quit smoking.

"Get me a lock of Bill's hair, and I'll get him to quit smoking," Orsini said.

"Lee, I can't do that, I'll get fired."

"Then I'll slip into his office and do it."

"If you go in there with the scissors, honey, you'll be thrown out of this office."

Orsini asked Phoebe to get her a lock of McArthur's hair three or four more times, but each time Phoebe refused. The two began joking about it, calling it their "double whammy."

Phoebe often told Orsini, "Your double whammy isn't working. I'm still gaining weight."

The week of July 2, 1982, Orsini and Phoebe talked frequently on the telephone about a wedding Tiffany was going to be in and other matters pertaining to their personal lives. They even planned to attend a rock concert together that week but didn't because they couldn't get tickets. During one of these idle conversations, Phoebe mentioned that the McArthur children were away at camp.

The only other person I have told this to besides Bill is Chris Piazza of the prosecutor's office because everything was so crazy, I didn't want them to think I was crazy too.... He called me and asked if Lee had any cats, and I said she has three or four cats. 'Do you know anything about her being involved in witchcraft?' he said, and I told him about the double whammy business.

I have heard that she is a witch, the head witch in a coven. Another thing, everything happened in intervals of six weeks—six, six, six. Now, I don't like Yankee Hall, but when he said he felt he was under a spell, I would not doubt that in the least bit. Just like I was. She had me so confused, which was her intention, so I could not figure out it was her doing these things. It's almost like you could not break away from her.

. . . Phoebe Jones Pinkston, 1984

Chapter Eight

"WE'RE TIGHTER THAN FAMILY," WAS Alice's favorite way of referring to her closest friends, those couples she had renamed the "Four Seasons" after the 1981 movie. She combined the seasons to come up with seasonal names for everyone: Tom and Beverly Brewer were known as the Fautumns; Bob and Beth Fowler were the Autmers, Karen and Al Colgrove were the Wintings, and John and Peggy Walls were the Sprummers. Alice and Bill were A plus and B minus Sumtum. Their names were a spin-off of Alice's days as a teacher.

The first day Beverly Brewer met Alice, Beverly had just come from her college graduation. It was 1977, and Beverly was thirty-seven years old, a little mature for a recent grad, but Beverly had reared her children and been through a divorce and remarriage, so education had been put on the back burner awhile. Alice respected education and Beverly's determination in getting one.

Beth and Beverly had been friends for many years, and Beth wanted to attend Beverly's graduation ceremony, but Beverly wouldn't let her because she was embarrassed about making a big deal out of her graduation since she was about fifteen years older than most of the other graduates. In fact, if it weren't for her husband's insistence she go through commencement, Beverly would have been satisfied with a diploma in her mailbox. But Tom Brewer didn't want his wife to miss anything. He wanted her to go through the cap and gown ceremony and get a class ring. Beverly finally relented and agreed to attend graduation, but she drew the line at inviting guests. She agreed to meet the Fowlers after commencement for drinks, and that's when Beverly met Beth's friend Alice McArthur.

Petite, almost five feet tall, with a gregarious personality and animated features, Beverly was an actress. She had never performed in anything other than local community theater, but she loved acting, and enjoyed entertaining her friends with her talents.

Perhaps that was why she and Alice became so close, because Alice liked to entertain and amuse her friends too—but in a much more personal way. Alice never sought attention in a public forum; she liked her privacy too much for that. She wasn't the type to perform on the stage, but she was the kind of woman who valued friends and wanted to make them happy, so she often performed for them at informal gatherings. Most of the time these gatherings were held at the Fowlers' cottage on Lake Hamilton in Hot Springs, about an hour's drive from Little Rock.

Hot Springs is known for its hot mineral waters that come steaming out of the ground, its bathhouses and horseracing track. As recently as the mid-1960s, Hot Springs was a gambler's haven. Although gambling was illegal, it went on openly in the spa city. State and local law enforcement officials knew about it, the citizenry knew about it, even the Democratic governor knew about it, but it was allowed to exist because it meant money and jobs. In the 1930s, Al Capone vacationed in the area, adding a little spice to the town's illegal legacy. It took a Republican governor to change things. In 1967 Winthrop Rockefeller, the first Republican governor of the state since Reconstruction, closed down gambling in Hot Springs.

Even without gambling, Hot Springs retained its popularity as a resort because of its large lakes and hot baths. Many Little Rock couples have summer cottages there, and it was a favorite meeting place for the McArthurs and their friends.

Not long after meeting Alice, Beverly and Tom Brewer saw the McArthurs at the Fowlers' cottage. Although Beverly liked to tease her friends and have them pop remarks back at her, she thought Alice's manner of joking was a little crude.

When she and her husband left the Fowlers', she turned to him and said, "You know, a little bit of Alice goes a long way." And her husband agreed.

But it didn't take any time for Beverly to change her mind about Alice. When Beverly finally realized Alice's taunting remarks were aimed at getting a reaction out of her, Beverly knew how to respond: "Hey, get off my ass, bitch," Beverly shot back at Alice one afternoon. That was all it took. From that moment on, Alice and Beverly were friends.

Beth Fowler first became acquainted with Alice through a bridge club, right after Alice's first child was born. The bridge club was made up of Alice's bowling partners. Beth was invited to go on an overnight bowling trip with the women, but they warned her to watch out for Alice because she would undoubtedly pull some prank at midnight.

At midnight Alice disappeared, and a few minutes later she entered from the hallway, wearing a garbage sack and a crazy-looking hat. She did a dance to the tune of "The Stripper," a comical, good-natured dance that broke the ice and set the tone for the remainder of the trip.

These three women—Alice, Beverly and Beth—were the nucleus of the Seasons, and Alice often referred to them as the Three Musketeers. They had so much fun together that Alice often remarked, "We could have fun at the dump."

Having been raised in south Louisiana in Cajun country, Alice enjoyed good food and drink. She often entertained at home and cooked her native Creole dishes of crawfish, shrimp and red beans and rice. When at Beth's or Beverly's lake houses on the weekend, Alice might have a bloody Mary in the morning, but she rarely drank during the day. Come 5 p.m., she would have a cocktail or two before dinner, but if the Seasons were partying, Alice could drink steadily without anyone noticing she had consumed much alcohol until late in the evening.

Alice, whose car bore a "CAJUN" personalized license plate, was typically Cajun—private, lover of family life, lover of good times and one who enjoyed sharing with her friends. She had a very low voice, and most people mistook her for a man on the telephone. She was not a classic beauty, but she was beautiful in her own way. She had tan, smooth, firm skin, warm gray eyes and light brown hair she frosted when she started seeing hints of gray. She was extremely neat. She ironed everything she wore, even her jeans, and she once told Beverly and Beth that when she taught school, it was the children who looked the neatest who usually were the smartest and did the best in school. "My children are going to look neat," she said, so she ironed everything they wore, too.

After getting together for bridge over a period of several years, Alice finally suggested to Beth they get their husbands together. This was a short time after Alice found out about McArthur's affair with Ms. X, and she was trying to better her marriage by expanding their social life to include more of each other. The first thing they did was attend an Arkansas Razorback football game. After the game they went to a well-known Little Rock night spot called Cajun's Wharf.

McArthur and Beth were sitting at a table near the dance floor, and Alice was dancing with Bob Fowler, when Beth noticed an exchange of words between Bob and two men on the other side of the dance floor. The song ended, and Bob escorted Alice back to her chair, took his wristwatch off, and headed back across the floor.

"What's going on?" Beth asked.

Alice hit the table with her hands and said, "Bill, fight, Bill, fight!"

By that time, one of the men at the other table had jumped up and swung at Bob, but the punch missed its mark. Beth, frightened and embarrassed, grabbed her coat and was headed for the door when Alice pulled her back. McArthur was making his way across the dance floor to help Bob, and Alice was cheering him on.

By the time the bouncers broke up the fight, McArthur had a mashed finger and a few bruises, but Bob came through the ruckus unscathed. Alice was as excited as a schoolgirl who had just cheered the star quarterback on to victory. She ridiculed Beth for trying to run away and kept talking about the incident the rest of the night, obviously very proud of her husband.

When Alice told Bill to fight, he jumped up immediately. Anything she wanted, Bill did. That's what has been so hard for everybody to understand. Here is this woman who was not softly feminine or beautiful or openly sexy, and Bill worshipped her. I think he did things that were foreign to him to make Alice happy. Alice didn't want him to be a candy ass; she wanted him, at times, to forget being the slick lawyer and be the man she married . . . under all that facade was what Alice loved in him.

. . . Beth Fowler, 1984

Chapter Nine

IN SOME WAYS, ALICE MCARTHUR WAS THE essence of the unfulfilled, middle-aged woman, yet in other ways she was totally satisfied. It was her womanhood, her role as mother that gave her the greatest happiness. But she hungered for something more, and comments she made to friends indicated that she felt time had run out for her. Whatever dreams she had ever dreamed, whatever goals she had hoped to reach, whatever opportunities she may have had, Alice seemed to feel they were beyond her grasp by the summer of 1982. Perhaps she could have somehow reconciled the part of her that was the nurturing, loving wife and mother with the part of her that was independent, aggressive and goal-oriented. It seems apparent that in July 1982, Alice McArthur was busy dealing with these different aspects of her personality, but she never forgot her friends.

Alice committed herself totally to her friends and family. Loyalty was important to her, and her husband's unfaithfulness hurt her deeply, but she never told her friends about his affair with Ms. X. She believed a woman should stand behind her husband, no matter what.

Alice's friends could see that Bill McArthur admired his wife, regardless of whatever domestic problems they had. She was the decision maker, and that was the way her husband wanted it. While relaxing by the pool at their home one Saturday, McArthur remarked to his friends, "I like Alice making the decisions. I make them all day, I carry people's problems all day long, and it's great to come home and have Alice say, 'Get your clothes on, we're going someplace.' That's great."

The first thing in the morning, as soon as the children left for school, Alice was on the telephone to call one or more of her friends. By 7:30 a.m. she had already read the paper, had a couple of cups of coffee, and sent Robyn and Chuck to school. As soon as she made the beds and washed the dishes, she would get out of the house. She disliked housework and was not the type of woman who devoted the whole day to it. She loved games, games that made her think, and everything she did, she did with full force, including playing tennis, a game she especially enjoyed.

In addition to games, Alice liked to stage plays featuring her friends. Once the Seasons decided to produce their own version of "Snow White and the Seven Dwarfs." The couples staged the show at one of their homes on the afternoon of a televised Arkansas-Texas football game. Arkansas football fans support the University of Arkansas Razorbacks as seriously as Dallas supports its Cowboys, and the Seasons never missed getting together for a game.

A few weeks before the game, they put the cast members' names into a hat and drew to see who would get which part. Alice wound up playing the mirror, and McArthur played a squirrel.

In preparation for the event they printed programs with the names of all the cast and characters. Some of the husbands got so involved in the project they spent several afternoons at the local hobby shop finding masks, glasses, funny hats and noses to make themselves look like dwarfs. As the big day approached, everyone got increasingly excited, but Alice and Bill never said a word except when the names were drawn and Beth Fowler picked Snow White: "Don't let Beth

be Snow White, she'll eat the whole apple!,"
McArthur teased because he knew Beth was always
complaining about being overweight.

By the time the Saturday of the football game arrived, all the costumes had been previewed but the
McArthurs'. As soon as the football game ended, the
couples put on their costumes and gathered in the den,
waiting to see what Alice and Bill would wear. Alice
came out of the bedroom all wrapped up in aluminum
foil, and Bill entered dressed in an old pillowcase into
which he had cut neck and armholes. On the front of
the pillow case was a little pouch filled with pecans and
on the front of the pouch he had written "Squirrel's
Nuts."

James Nelson, another member of the Seasons, was
dressed in a witch hat and carried a broom. As the
play began, he looked at Alice and delivered his lines:
"Mirror, mirror on the wall, who's the fairest one of
all?"

"That Goddamn Snow White is!" Alice replied.

"Where is the little bitch?"

"She's shacked up in the woods with seven funny
little men."

So went the Seasons' slightly bawdy version of
"Snow White." It was one of many good times together they would always remember, despite whatever
else might pull them apart.

In 1981 country-western dancing was the rage all
across the nation, and Little Rock was no exception.
Alice's friends wanted to learn these dances, but they
had to talk her into it. They hired an instructor to give
them lessons one night each week, taking turns using a
different couple's garage. Alice didn't like that type of
music, and she told her friends they would never see
her in western clothes. But Alice gradually changed
her mind.

After learning the dances, the couples ventured out

to the Kountry Klub Kowboy Disco, the club owned by Bob Troutt. Soon Alice was enjoying dancing the Cotton-eyed Joe, and McArthur and James Nelson started talking about opening a night club of their own.

"I'm going to go along with it. It's something Bill has always wanted to do, but I don't want it to take him away from his family," Alice told Beverly Brewer.

"Now Alice, it's going to take him away from his family for awhile," Beverly responded.

"I can handle that, but I'm not going to have my children suffer," Alice said.

The opening of BJ's Star Studded Honky Tonk in December 1981 was something in which all the McArthurs' friends participated. They bought boots and hats and western wear for the occasion, and Alice wound up owning a dozen of the western-styled shirts she once considered tasteless. The day before the grand opening, the Seasons went out to the club and helped set up tables and decorations. Afterward, Alice sent hand-lettered thank-you cards to her friends.

At about the same time, Alice learned she would be receiving payments from oil leases in Louisiana. The money was a result of her inheritance of a half-interest in a seventy-acre tract of oil-producing land in Pointe Coupee Parish, northwest of Baton Rouge. About fifteen acres was producing oil and was located on what is known as the Tuscaloosa Trend, an oil-bearing geological formation beginning in Alabama and extending well into Louisiana. Prior to 1982, Alice received only about $5,000 annually from the leases, but in January 1982 she received about $25,000 and was told her checks could increase to between $25,000 and $30,000 per month. Although Alice never realized such handsome royalties because the wells were soon closed for repair and never reopened, she was worried about how she would handle that much money. She told this to her friend Karen Colgrove sometime in March or

April when they were discussing Bill's involvement in
BJ's.

"I haven't told Bill that the checks might end up
being that much," Alice said.

"My God, Alice, I just can't imagine having that
kind of income," Karen exclaimed.

"He wants to make some money for us in this club,
and he has worked so hard, how can I go and say,
'Look, get out of the club, we don't need the money. I
have it.' I can't take that away from Bill. I can't burst
his bubble," Alice said.

Alice was worried the money might change their
lives. She didn't want a bigger house; she just wanted
to redecorate the one she had. She didn't want things
to change.

"I don't want to spoil the kids with this money
either," she told Karen, "I'm going to talk to an attorney and have all the money go directly to the attorney and let him invest it for me. I'll just put
myself on an allowance. I don't want this money
ruining our lives. Maybe I'll do a couple of crazy
things, but nothing big," she said. "In the meantime,
I'll let Bill have his fun with the club for a few years.
He needs that for himself."

"I still can't imagine that kind of income coming in
every month," Karen said. "It's scary."

"Yes, it is scary, very scary," Alice said.

Alice and her friends had been planning a trip to Ft.
Walton, Florida for months. In preparation for the
trip, she sent out newsletters written in her careful
script. The first such "Four Seasons Female Newsletter" was dated March 24, and addressed to the "Seasonal Ladies."

Alice decreed in her newsletter a "two-piece bathing
suit is not only necessary, but compulsory and manda-
tory, if one is planning a Florida vacation." She called
herself "The Committee" and told the others, "The
fact that there are a few bodies in the above mentioned

list that should not be found dead in one so-named suit
cannot deter any member from following Committee
instructions."

In addition to a two-piece bathing suit, a razor was
required for the trip because, "You are not nor will
pretend to be European ladies." She told the women
all items such as soap, shampoo, deodorant, and co-
lognes would be checked military fashion upon arrival
by the Special Commander's Committee Appointee,
Bunny Winting, who would reprimand those who
broke the "Seasonal" rules. The newsletter continued:

"Thank you for your cooperation. Do not think that
the entire vacation will be conducted Gestapo fashion.
It is simply that a highly organized level of disorgani-
zation is difficult to maintain among consenting adults.
We must continue our state of inefficiency and affabil-
ity at all costs."

Finally, Alice wrote: "If you haven't paid much attention to your body lately, chances are no one else has
either."

Alice sent her second "Four Seasons Female Newsletter" out on April 29. This time much of the news
was devoted to a breakdown of the anticipated expenses. Alice was very sensitive to the fact that not all
the Seasonal Ladies had a lot of disposable income. So
they could all go, she wrote, "The following financial
report will help some of you pilfer from your children's
savings."

Regarding the two-piece bathing suits, Alice said,
"It has been brought to the attention of the committee
that several Seasons have not yet purchased two-piece
bathing suits. Therefore, a fine figure of a Seasonal
Lady, Boom Boom Autmer, has been appointed to be
First Deputy Assistant to the Special Commander's
Committee Appointee, Commandant Bunny Winting.
This appointment was necessitated by the fact that
Bunny is frequently blitzed, and Boom Boom will

offer a pleasing balance with her Tara sophistication to check out all suits."

Alice planned a picnic at her house on Friday, May 21, a day she called "Sun Day." Those going on the Florida trip would bring a sack lunch and make final preparations and discuss clothing, but May 21 was the day Alice's car blew up.

Alice was really an introvert. She liked to sit around reading poetry, other literature, listen to music.

. . . William C. "Bill" McArthur, 1984

Chapter Ten

WITH THE CLUB RUNNING SMOOTHLY BY the late spring of 1982, McArthur began turning his attention back to his law practice. He had a big trial coming in May concerning the Browning Arms Company. McArthur represented a dentist who was hunting in Montana and claimed his Browning shotgun discharged accidentally, blew off his right thumb and index finger and ended his dental career. The plaintiff's team included McArthur, an attorney from Louisiana and one from California.

The out-of-town attorneys checked into the downtown Little Rock Holiday Inn. Every day after the trial, the attorneys met at the motel in an extra room they rented for a conference room to prepare for the next day's session.

On the morning of May 21, McArthur went to the office a little early so he could return a few telephone calls and pick up some papers he needed for court. One of the messages Phoebe had left for him was a call from Lee Orsini. He returned Orsini's call, and shortly after 8 a.m. Alice called him to tell him a bomb had gone off underneath her car.

"What do you mean a bomb?," he asked.

"I started to drive off, and there was an explosion," Alice said, almost out of breath from the excitement.

"Are you hurt?" McArthur asked, thinking Alice must be mistaken, it couldn't have been a bomb. Perhaps there was something wrong with her car.

"No, there's just some nicks on my leg."

"Is someone there with you?"

"Yes."

"I'll be right home," he said.

When he got home, the police were there, news people had already gathered, and Alice was inside the house with a neighbor. She told her husband her car exploded as she was easing it out of the driveway on her way to play tennis. The floor beneath her feet buckled from the explosion, which caused only minor damage to the car.

They learned later that the bomb, which had been made from a battery, a shampoo bottle, a cigar box, a blasting cap and a water gel explosive, had only partially detonated. According to a report made by federal Alcohol, Tobacco and Firearm agents, it appeared that the device was placed under the car by lodging it between the frame and the emergency brake cable, directly under the driver's seat. The agents reported they suspected that a string was attached between a toggle switch on the bomb and the front tire of the car. Thus, as the car moved forward, the string tightened, pulling the toggle switch to the "on" position, closing the circuit and setting off the blasting cap. However, the cap did not set off the explosive. If it had exploded with full force, it would have blown both Alice and her 1977 Oldsmobile Cutlass to pieces.

McArthur suggested she go to the doctor to make sure her injuries were not serious, but before she left, an officer asked her who she thought might have planted a bomb in her car. She replied, "Bob Troutt."

The fifty-three-year-old Troutt had gained a tough reputation during his years as a nightclub owner. The day before Alice's car was bombed, he had been charged with arranging to have three businesses burned, including BJ's. Troutt had closed his club the previous month.

After Alice left, the assistant Little Rock police

chief, Jess F. Hale, arrived. Known to everyone he worked with as "Doc," he and McArthur had known each other for years. Hale was a different kind of cop. McArthur knew that from working as a defense attorney fifteen years. Hale had worked his way up through the ranks of the Little Rock Police Department into his current position, and McArthur knew he could be trusted always to act professionally and tell the truth. The two men first met each other when McArthur was fresh out of law school and Hale was a patrolman, a time when McArthur was frequently appointed to defend people who couldn't afford lawyers. McArthur was in the courtroom all the time, and he would either run into Hale in the courtroom or in the small courthouse coffee shop.

Hale and McArthur admired each other's professionalism. McArthur respected Hale's ability as an investigator, and Hale respected the lawyer's skill in the courtroom. In the early years, if McArthur beat Hale on a case, the lawyer would tell him where he thought the police had made a mistake. And if McArthur lost, he held no resentment. When the two men faced each other during a trial, they knew they were facing the best the opposition could offer.

Hale talked to the officers who were already present at the McArthur house, and they told him what little they knew about the bombing. They also told him what Alice had said about Troutt. Hale asked McArthur, who was standing near Alice's damaged Oldsmobile, if he agreed with Alice that Troutt was behind the bombing.

"No, I don't. My instinct tells me no," McArthur said.

"Why?" Hale asked.

"Because there's so much heat on him now, he would have to know that he would be the first one looked at; and, secondly, unless there was some monumental blunder here, I think he would go against me, not against my family. I think it has something to do with the Ron Orsini case."

"Why do you think that, Bill?"

"Because so much crazy stuff has happened in that thing, something has happened continuously since his death, somebody shot at Lee Orsini, somebody broke into her house and all that, just continuously things keep happening."

Pulaski County Prosecuting Attorney Wilbur C. "Dub" Bentley told the media the bombing could be related to several ongoing cases, including the investigation of Bob Troutt and the murder of Ron Orsini. He said he was concerned for the safety of Mary Lee Orsini, Bill McArthur and Tommy Robinson.

Robinson announced he was initiating an investigation into organized crime in Arkansas and said the Troutt, Orsini and McArthur cases could all be the result of a "movement in organized crime to take over Arkansas" or a "power struggle" among local crime figures. He said he would talk with authorities from Louisiana about the activities of the chief of organized crime in New Orleans, a purported Mafia chieftain.

The Four Seasons Female Newsletters stopped after the bombing, and the trip was almost canceled. Alice called Beverly Brewer a couple of weeks before the trip:

"I don't know if I am going to be able to go to Florida."

"Oh, Alice, you need to go."

"I'm worried about Bill and my babies. I'm going to ask you a favor," Alice said. "Can Bill and my kids and Bill's parents stay in your lake house while we're in Florida? We'll pay you for it."

"No, you will not. You don't think another thing of it. The house is yours, that's a wonderful idea. Nobody will know where they are, and you're safe and secure and won't have to worry about Bill."

The women planned to leave before sunrise to begin their drive to Florida. In the days leading up to the trip Alice teased Beverly about her typically theatrical unwillingness to get up early: "Little Bitch will have to stay up and party all night." But when Alice arrived in the borrowed van to pick up Beverly, she was dressed and ready to go.

After Alice picked up each of the travelers, they exchanged presents they had brought along for each other. Alice gave them all cigarette lighters and insulated beer can holders.

They weren't even out of Arkansas before they had to stop to go to the bathroom. It was daylight, and they had already drunk their first beers, but they made a rule that the person next in line to drive could not drink anything alcoholic for two hours before her driving shift. They had enough food for ten times their number, and they ate and drank all the way to Florida, about twelve hours.

Once they arrived at the rented condo, they drew numbers to see who would sleep where. Beth was worried about the sleeping arrangements. She had never slept with anyone but her husband before, and she hated the idea of sleeping in the hide-a-bed in the living room because she liked to retire early. Beverly and Alice arranged the numbers so that Beth had to sleep in the hide-a-bed with Alice. Alice liked to stay up and talk all night, and they knew this arrangement would disturb Beth.

After getting a few laughs out of Beth's distress, Beverly and Alice admitted they had rigged the drawing and agreed to draw numbers all over again, but it came out the same way, with Beth and Alice in the hide-a-bed.

They slept until about 9:30 a.m., cooked breakfast and then took a few beers down to the beach for a couple of hours until lunchtime when they went back to the condo to eat sandwiches and watch soap operas.

Some would then take naps. Alice always wrote in a diary she referred to as "The Florida Chronicle," and she kept trying to get the others to write in it. Later in the afternoon, they cleaned up and went shopping or out to eat.

One afternoon when Karen went shopping with Alice, Karen found a bathing suit she really liked and tried it on. Alice asked her, "Are you gonna buy that bathing suit?"

"Yes, I am," Karen said.

"It'll mess up your budget, won't it?" Alice asked, sincerely concerned Karen might run short of money before the end of the vacation.

"No, Alice, it'll be all right, really."

Alice reached in her purse and took out forty dollars and gave it to Karen. Karen tried to hand it back to her, but Alice wouldn't take it. After the trip, Karen gave her a check to repay her, but Alice never cashed it.

The trip to Florida was a relaxing time for all of them, especially Alice, who had been under a lot of strain since the bombing. Although she had not let her fear show, it was there like an undercurrent, quietly waiting to snatch her away.

Toward the end of their week-long trip, they were beginning to get on each other's nerves a bit, and one night Alice and Karen got into an argument during dinner. By the time they returned to the condo from the restaurant, Alice had tears in her eyes.

"Alice, calm down. Let's don't mess up the trip," Beverly told her, thinking Alice was still angry at Karen.

"Damn, Beverly. Somebody's trying to kill me, and I'm so fucking scared."

Beverly tried to comfort her, "I can't tell you I know how you feel because I don't know."

"Goddamn it, who would want to kill me?"

"In my mind, I'm still trying to tell myself someone's trying to scare you, to scare Bill."

"I just don't know," Alice replied, hitting the wall with her fist.

Alice was not comfortable around strangers at all. She liked to have a fairly small group of friends, and she knew exactly where she stood with them. You put her in a situation around people she did not know well, and she seldom said anything.

. . . William C. "Bill" McArthur, 1984

Chapter Eleven

ON MONDAY, JUNE 29, 1982, A COUPLE OF weeks after the Florida trip, Alice and Bill McArthur drove their two children forty-five miles to summer camp. After dropping off the children, they enjoyed a leisurely drive back to Little Rock, the first of many quiet times they spent with each other that week.

Each night they either went out to dinner together or cooked something on the grill in their backyard by the pool. One evening they drove to an out-of-town car dealership to look at vans. Their time together was special that week. This was the most time they had spent together in years. But the Fourth of July week-end was going to be a little different. It marked the end of the McArthurs' week-long honeymoon, and they planned to spend the weekend at the Brewers' lakehouse in Hot Springs.

The Brewers' lakehouse was across the lake from the Fowlers'. All the other times McArthur and Alice went to the lake with their friends, there were from eight to twenty children present, but this time there would be none. This weekend the adults could relax and not spend the entire time pulling children behind ski boats, lighting firecrackers and issuing warnings to be careful with the Roman candles.

On Thursday, July 1, McArthur and Phoebe went to lunch together; and when they got back to the office, Alice was sitting behind Bill's desk leaning back in his chair, her feet propped up in front of her. She was dressed in her usual summer attire of shorts and tennis shoes. McArthur kissed her on the cheek, and Phoebe asked about her recent trip to Florida. Alice told Phoebe some of the crazy things she and her girlfriends did while on vacation and asked Phoebe to make a copy of a small book she had put together which contained funny things her friends said while on the trip. Alice wanted to give each woman a copy as a souvenir. Phoebe made copies of the book and gave them to Alice. Then Alice and Bill left together to look at more vans.

After the shopping trip Bill returned to his office, and Alice stopped by Karen Colgrove's house to show Karen some newly developed photographs of the Florida trip. They hugged because they hadn't seen each other since the trip. Karen had been out of town with her family and just returned. Alice told her what a wonderful week she and Bill were having and said they were enjoying being together, just the two of them. Alice was in great spirits and invited Karen and Al to go out to dinner that evening, but Karen declined. They talked about going to the lake for the Fourth of July and discussed food for the trip, and Karen told Alice if she wanted to get an early start and ride with her she could, but Alice said she was thinking about waiting and riding to the lake with Bill.

On Friday, July 2, Peggy Walls asked Alice to go to Hot Springs with her early in the day so they could go shopping together, but Alice again declined an early ride.

McArthur was scheduled to represent a doctor in municipal court Friday at 10 a.m. He got out of court shortly before noon and called Phoebe from a pay telephone at the courthouse to let her know he was on his way back to the office. When he arrived, another client was waiting to see him, so McArthur suggested the two men grab a quick hamburger.

Orsini had been calling Phoebe all week to set up an appointment with McArthur. One was scheduled for Tuesday, but Orsini canceled it and asked Phoebe to reschedule it for Wednesday. But Phoebe told her McArthur was in a jury trial Wednesday, and Thursday was already booked. On Friday morning Orsini again called Phoebe about getting in to see McArthur, and Phoebe tentatively scheduled an appointment for 4:30 p.m. but told Orsini to call her later to confirm it.

Phoebe left the office while McArthur and his client were at lunch and walked down the street to a gas station to buy a soft drink. When she returned, McArthur was talking to Alice on the phone.

"We can either go after we leave the club tonight or wait and drive over in the morning. . . . Well, we could just pack up and leave from the club. . . ."

After he hung up, Phoebe told him, "Lee wants to come in this afternoon."

"I'll work her in. I want to leave early," he said.

Phoebe called Orsini and explained that McArthur wanted to leave early and asked her to come in about 3:30.

McArthur was standing in front of Phoebe's desk when she hung up the phone. He had a handful of canned Diet Cokes. He put one on her desk, snapped the top off another and took a long gulp.

The phone buzzed as McArthur walked toward his office. She picked it up, "Yes, he's back. Just a minute." She punched the hold button and told McArthur who was holding.

As he picked up the receiver, McArthur called out to Phoebe, "Let's try to get everyone in and out as fast as we can this afternoon."

"We can try," Phoebe replied.

About 1:30 p.m. Alice called Beverly, who was already in Hot Springs, and said, "Don't go to the grocery store, I have a bunch of croissants and sweet rolls for breakfast, and I thought we would have red beans and rice for supper. I've got hot dogs for the people who don't want beans and rice. God, I can't believe I'm finally going to spend the night at the Brewers' lakehouse."

"I can't either," Beverly said, "You only get to spend the night with the Brewers when you don't have children with you."

"There's a tennis tournament on TV this weekend I want to watch," Alice said.

"Am I going to have to watch that damn TV tennis?"

"Yes," Alice said.

"Well, would you take the TV set in the bathroom?," Beverly joked.

Then Beverly asked Alice if she intended to ride to Hot Springs that afternoon with the Colgroves.

"I would, but there's only one thing that bothers me. I hate for Bill to be on the road that late by himself. It's his night to work at the club."

"Yeah, that's scary," Beverly said.

"Bill's coming home about 4:30 or 5:00 to mow the yard. If I'm not here, he won't mow it." Beverly laughed at that. She knew Alice was right. Husbands sometimes had to be pushed into getting things done around the house. Beverly's husband was the same way.

"Well," Alice continued, "the big thing is Bill working at the club tonight, and that would mean he would be driving by himself. It might be ten o'clock, it might be midnight. I'm going to go out there with Bill, and we'll leave from there. It might be late. Will that bother you?"

"Yeah, I want you here," Beverly said. "Seriously, though, no. If I'm in bed, I'm in bed. If I'm up we'll have a drink and a smoke."

* * *

While Lee Orsini waited to see McArthur, she and Phoebe talked about an Elton John concert. Their plans to attend it fell through because an hour after the ticket office opened that morning all tickets were sold out.

While they talked, Orsini asked Phoebe if she could use the telephone to call her mother. Phoebe told her to use the phone on her desk, and while Orsini dialed the number, Phoebe walked into the kitchen for one of the cans of Diet Coke McArthur had put in the refrigerator.

"I can't believe this! I can't remember my own mother's phone number," Orsini told the receptionist, after dialing the phone several times.

It was about 3:40 p.m. when Phoebe left the office for the day, leaving Orsini and several other clients in the waiting room. The receptionist noted that Orsini finally got to see McArthur about 4:30 p.m.

Orsini entered McArthur's office and closed the door behind her before telling him she had met a man who was interested in buying BJ's. She said the man told her he had contacted her because her husband, Ron, had done some air conditioning work for him. The man's name was "Hale," and he worked for the Southland Corporation, she told McArthur. She said the reason the man contacted her instead of McArthur was because the man had read newspaper accounts of her association with McArthur as a result of the grand jury's investigation of Ron's death.

"Look, Lee, the FBI is investigating the bombing of Alice's car, and they're very suspicious of anything concerning the club. You told me once before about someone who was interested in the club, and I passed that name along to the feds, in case the bombing is somehow tied in with the club. But they keep wanting to know who is furnishing me with these names. I haven't told them who it is, but I'm going to have to give them your name," he said.

"Well for heavens sake! I can't imagine why," Orsini exclaimed.

McArthur hated to tell her what the FBI agent had told him, but he felt he owed her that much, as her attorney. He didn't want her to think he didn't trust her, but he felt obliged to cooperate with the FBI, no matter how off base he thought they were regarding his client. Finally he blurted it out, "Because they think you're somehow involved in the car bombing."

Displeasure immediately registered on Orsini's face. "That's the most ridiculous thing in the world. Why would they think that?" she asked, visibly shaken.

"I agree it's ridiculous; I'm only telling you what they told me. Now, I have to tell them. . . ."

"Oh, Bill, don't be silly, just tell them about the attorney/client thing . . . you know, tell them it's a client who. . . ."

"That's what I said, but they keep asking," he said.

Orsini got up to leave: "You can handle them, Bill. Just refuse to tell them. God knows I don't want to borrow any more trouble. Now, promise me, you won't tell them I told you about Hale."

"We'll see, we'll see," McArthur replied. "I'll do what I can."

Mary was a greedy person. She likes to put on airs. I knew her for lots of years, I knew how she acted, very sly, very greedy, very vindictive, very devious. I wouldn't put anything past her, I really wouldn't.

. . . Ron Hatcher, Lee Orsini's brother, 1984

Chapter Twelve

JULY 2, 1982, WAS A TYPICALLY HOT AND humid Arkansas summer day—the kind that makes bare skin stick to leather automobile upholstery. When McArthur left his air-conditioned office, sultry waves of heat rolled over him. He unlocked and opened the door to his Buick and got a blast of heat in his face.

He tossed his jacket into the car and loosened his necktie. By the time he had inserted the key into the ignition, he already had the air conditioning turned up full blast, aiming the vents at his face and neck.

He traveled his regular route home—Little Rock's Wilbur Mills Expressway, named after one of the state's most illustrious sons, to Interstate 430, which runs north and south along the edge of Pleasant Valley. Traffic was thick. Workers trying to get an early start on the holiday weekend had clogged the lanes, and when he got off at the Rodney Parham exit, he had to sit through two lights before making a left turn toward Pleasant Valley. His thoughts that broiling afternoon were racing between the club and the lake. He was looking forward to a relaxing weekend.

By the time he pulled into the steep, semicircular driveway in front of his split-level home at 24 Inverness Circle, McArthur had decided he and Alice would first grab a bite to eat at El Patio, a Mexican restaurant owned by their friends, John and Peggy Walls, then go to the club for a few hours before heading to

Hot Springs. He figured it would be long past midnight by the time they arrived at the Brewers' lakehouse.

About 5:10 p.m., McArthur parked his car behind Alice's Cutlass. He noticed Boo—short for Bourgeois—the family's toy poodle, scampering across the yard, jumping and spinning a wag-tail welcome to her master. He thought it was a little unusual for the dog to be out, but he knew she could have slipped outside any number of ways. He picked her up and carried her back into the house through the front door. As he entered the house, he noticed several sacks of groceries sitting inside the split-foyer to the left of the front door. He heard the television on downstairs in the den and, assuming Alice was there on the couch taking a nap, he went upstairs past the kitchen, where he saw a large baked ham sitting on the kitchen counter, past the living room and down the hall toward the master bedroom.

The McArthurs had been remodeling their home and were converting an upstairs bedroom into a large closet and storage area for Bill. He took the suit coat he had worn all day and tossed it over a rack in his closet, then proceeded down the hall, into the master bedroom. There he saw clothing stacked on the bed in preparation for packing into suitcases for the trip to the lake.

It was a large room with lots of furniture. A chest of drawers was on the right side of the entrance and on the other side of the chest of drawers was a door leading to a bathroom. On the far side of the room, across from the entrance, was a sliding glass door that led to a deck on the back of the house. To the left of the room's entrance stood a large desk. The door to the bedroom closet was to the left of the desk, and an ironing board stood near the foot of the bed between the bed and desk, slightly blocking the path to the closet.

As was his custom when he got home from work, McArthur stopped at the dresser and emptied his pockets—cigarette lighter, keys and money—onto the dresser. Then he turned and noticed the new shorts

Alice had bought lying on the bed. He almost stopped to try them on but instead he turned and walked out of the bedroom. He went back down the hallway, down the stairs and into the den.

"Honey, I'm home," he called.

There was no answer. He saw Alice's cigarettes and lighter on the end table next to the couch and her shoes on the floor. Not finding her napping on the couch aroused his curiosity. He went into the gameroom next to the den but didn't see her there either. He looked into the garage which opens off the gameroom and went out into the yard. He checked both sides of the house, the front yard, and he called through the fence into the backyard by the pool. He got no reply.

An uneasy feeling came over him, as he went back into the house and out the back door, but she wasn't in the pool or lounging on the patio. He came back into the house again and proceeded upstairs and down the hallway toward the master bedroom for the second time. As he neared the bedroom door, he noticed damage to some new wallpaper at the end of the hall. He could hear the pounding of his heart inside his ears, and a queasy feeling grabbed at the pit of his stomach. The wallpaper had only been up a few days, but already it looked as if the paper had been torn or pulled away from the wall. As he looked closer, he could see what appeared to be a bullet hole in the groove in the wallboard.

That's when he became scared—absolutely scared to death. He panicked and hurried back to the kitchen to telephone the police. Since the car bombing, the whole family had tried to remain cautious. He had assumed the bomb was meant for him. Now the thought that someone had come to the house looking for him and found Alice alone terrified him. He thought Alice might have been kidnapped.

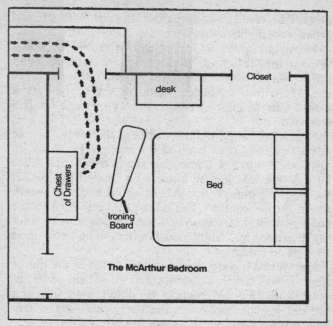

The McArthur Bedroom

He picked up the wall phone in the kitchen but couldn't get a dial tone. He ran downstairs to the telephone by the couch in the den. The phone was a portable, cordless model with a button that could be switched on the "on" position, and he clicked it on and ran back up to the kitchen telephone and dialed the only number he could remember for the Little Rock Police Department. It was one he had learned years before, but it was now a bondsman's office. The lady on the other end of the line gave him the correct number of the police department, and he quickly hung up and called it. After calling the police, McArthur called the Pulaski County Sheriff's Office because he had asked the sheriff's department to keep an eye on his house since the bombing. Sheriff Tommy Robinson and Major Larry Dill had agreed to investigate the bombing because they were already involved in an investigation of Bob Troutt and other local nightclub owners.

McArthur spoke to Major Dill, who said he would come to the McArthurs' home as soon as he could. Dill's office was on Roosevelt Road, about ten miles from the McArthur residence, and McArthur figured it would take at least fifteen to twenty minutes for Dill to arrive.

Next, he called Anita Prather, the only one of Alice's friends who lived close enough for Alice to have walked to her house, but she had not seen Alice all day. He told her he already had called the police, the dog was outside and Alice's shoes and purse were there, but he couldn't find Alice. Midway through the conversation, McArthur realized his desperate-sounding questions had frightened Prather, so he hung up as soon as he could.

He walked toward the front door again as the phone rang. It was Karen Colgrove, and he got rid of her as quickly as he could because he didn't want to alarm her the way he had Anita Prather. Within a few moments of that phone call, Anita Prather arrived.

Little Rock patrolman Robert McNeely received a call to a disturbance at 24 Inverness and arrived at the address at 5:31 p.m. He parked his patrol car in front of the house, walked down the steep driveway to the front door and knocked. McArthur came to the door and let McNeely in. McArthur told the patrolman he thought his wife had been kidnapped, and while they were talking, McNeely saw Mrs. Prather standing nearby.

"What makes you think she's been kidnapped?," McNeely asked.

"When I came home, the door was open and the dog was outside. The TV's on and I can't find her."

"Have you checked real good?"

"Yes, yes I have."

They walked upstairs, and McArthur showed McNeely the tear in the wallpaper.

"Do you know what this is?" McArthur asked, afraid to hear the officer's answer.

McNeely knew immediately the hole was made by a bullet, but McArthur looked pretty upset already, and McNeely didn't see any sense in upsetting him further. He didn't answer the question.

"Before we call out the troops," McNeely said, "let's check the house again and see if there's a note. Maybe she went off with a friend."

While the men were talking, Prather went into the darkened master bedroom and looked at the clothes on the bed, trying to reconstruct in her mind what she would do had she been Alice preparing for a weekend trip to the lake. She walked over by the ironing board which was standing between the bed and closet and happened to glance into the closet. She froze momentarily when she realized the form she saw sticking out from behind some clothes resembled human flesh, possibly legs. It only took a fraction of a second for Prather's mind to assimilate what she saw and jolt her body into action. She rushed back into the hall and told the men she thought she had found something. Officer McNeely entered the bedroom first, followed by Major Dill, who had arrived only moments earlier. Dill stopped at the doorway and prevented McArthur from following him into the room.

The patrolman looked into the closet, parting the clothing enough to reveal the lifeless body of Alice McArthur.

McNeely could tell she had been shot. He felt for a pulse on one wrist and on her neck, although he knew there probably would not be one, and he made mental note of what she was wearing—greenish-colored terry cloth shorts and top and several gold chains around her neck.

Dill and Prather led McArthur downstairs into the den. By this time McArthur realized his wife was hurt or worse, but nobody had told him she was dead. His mind was beginning to react to the stress. He felt that things were way out of his control. Sometime soon after, Prather called her husband, who was a doctor, told him about the body and told him to come to the McArthurs' as soon as he could.

McNeely's backup, Rick Edgar, was in his patrol car at the corner of Markham and Mississippi Street when he got the disturbance call to 24 Inverness. He was not in a hurry to get to the disturbance, and he took his time driving the four or five miles to the residence. When Edgar pulled his patrol car up to the house, he saw another Little Rock Police Department patrol car and several unmarked police cars already there. He recognized the unmarked cars as those used by the sheriff's department and wondered why they were there— usually they only respond to calls outside the city limits. This call was inside the city.

Edgar went inside. Several deputies were already there, but the only one he recognized was Major Dill. McNeely was in the bedroom on the telephone as Edgar entered the room. Edgar went between the ironing board and bed and over to the closet. He didn't know whose house he was in or who the woman in the closet was. He checked for a pulse and noticed the dead woman had a pen in her left hand.

Edgar walked away from the closet area as three sheriff's deputies came into the room. They went over to the closet and peered inside. Edgar asked what they were doing.

"We're looking for evidence," one of the men said.

"I think we need to wait until our detectives get here," he told them. Edgar knew McNeely was talking to headquarters, and he didn't want anyone to touch anything until his superiors arrived.

Two of the deputies had already positioned themselves on their knees in the closet. Edgar again told them to get out. All but one obeyed his orders. The last deputy remained in the closet, and Edgar walked over and grabbed the man's arm and said, "We're going to get out of here," and asked the man what he was doing.

"I'm looking for flowers," the man said.

"What are you looking for flowers for?" Edgar asked. But he never got a reply.

Edgar still didn't know whose house he was in until he ushered the deputies out of the bedroom and went downstairs. That's when he recognized McArthur, sitting on the couch in the den, crying. Although Edgar knew McArthur's reputation as a defense lawyer, he had only met him once, in a judge's chambers where the lawyer had questioned Edgar about a case. Edgar thought of McArthur as someone who was always in control. But McArthur wasn't in control now. He was crying and seemed unable to talk, and when Edgar offered him a cigarette, he couldn't light it himself, so Edgar lit it for him.

Al Dawson, the youngest son of eight children born to a sharecropper at Piggott, Arkansas, liked police work. He preferred it to working in a factory or gas station as he had done during his high school years. He knew the police department would offer educational opportunities as well as a steady income, so he signed on in 1973. By 1982, Dawson had become a detective, and was known by his superiors as a good investigator.

Dawson arrived on the scene after McNeely and Edgar and saw a plain gray sheriff's department car parked facing east on Inverness. He recognized Major Dill standing beside one of the unmarked cars talking to a man Dawson thought was Captain Bobby Woodward, but he couldn't be sure because he was too far away. As he approached the house, he noticed four or five additional deputies in and about the house.

Dawson wondered how so many deputies got there before he did. Why was the response time of the sheriff's department so much faster than that of his own department? He assumed there must have been unmarked units already in the area, but he knew this would have been unusual because most of the time those units stayed at headquarters, a fifteen-minute drive from 24 Inverness during rush-hour traffic. The Little Rock Police Department first responds to calls with a uniformed officer who will call non-uniformed people from headquarters as needed. Dawson reasoned to himself that since the bombing, the sheriff's office must have been keeping an eye on the McArthur place.

In truth, the May 21 blast created a chasm between the sheriff's office and the Little Rock police. Sheriff Robinson told reporters his office would not share information with any law enforcement agency other than the prosecuting attorney's office and the FBI. The sheriff said he was investigating the Orsini case, Troutt, the bombing and organized crime in Arkansas. Meanwhile, the Little Rock police chief said his department was the primary investigative agency in the bombing.

By the time Dawson arrived, Officer McNeely already had been told by his shift commander to secure the crime scene. Since McNeely and Edgar were both rookies, they felt a little intimidated by Major Dill's presence, realizing they would have to ask him to leave in order to preserve evidence as ordered. The rookies managed to get the deputies out of the house, but it was obvious to Dawson the deputies resented being thrown out. Nevertheless everyone was cleared out of the house, including McArthur, until the detectives arrived.

Edgar and McNeely turned the bedroom over to Dawson, and the two policemen stayed outside to keep other people from entering the house. They had specific orders to keep Sheriff Tommy Robinson out, but when he arrived, he didn't try to get past them. A short while later the police photographer arrived and was allowed to enter to take photos of the crime scene.

The photographer took pictures from several angles

in the closet. After first taking the photos of the clothes-filled closet, the police moved some of the hanging clothes to expose the entire body. According to police officers present that day, only part of Alice's legs could be seen without parting the clothes. The rest of the body was hidden from sight.

The body was underneath a thirty-six-inch-high shelf, sandwiched in between clothes hanging from a rod underneath the shelf. The trajectory of the bullet that killed Alice showed she had been facing away from her killer in a bent position when she was shot, evidently trying to get down behind the clothes in the closet to hide. One of the shots missed her entirely. The bullet was found on the closet floor. After the second shot, at the moment of death, the body slumped backward into the closet, hidden from casual view.

Police later theorized that when Alice first ran into the bedroom, the killer probably was no more than ten to fifteen steps behind her, and she must have realized there was not enough time to get the balcony door unlocked and get out that way. Hence, she ran to the closet, either to hide or to get a gun her husband kept there. The .38-caliber revolver was found in the closet at the very back of one of the higher shelves, above Alice's head.

After the news got out that Alice had been killed, reporters, judges, friends of the McArthur family, people from the prosecutor's office, and high-ranking law enforcement officials from several agencies began arriving. Even Little Rock Police Chief Walter E. "Sonny" Simpson came to the scene. Edgar and McNeely were having a hard time keeping people out of the house.

Dawson was beginning to get nervous about having so many people trample all over his crime scene. It seemed like every supervisor from every police agency was on hand. Although most of the photographs were taken before people started arriving, Dawson felt it was the worst-managed situation he had ever witnessed. Some officers were running around talking about suspects even before Dawson and his men finished working the scene. Later that evening, federal Alcohol, Tobacco and Firearms agents showed up at the crime scene carrying photos of a thug named Eugene James "Yankee" Hall.

Some of the officers at the scene knew that just hours before Alice's murder, Bob Troutt had called the LRPD and told them a "salt and pepper" team—one white and one black man—would try to kill her. He said he received his information from North Little Rock policeman T.J. Farley, who had investigated the Ron Orsini homicide. Troutt's reason for notifying LRPD was he knew he would be a possible suspect if anything happened to her, especially since his name had been mentioned in connection with the bombing, but nobody took Troutt's tip seriously. No effort was made to warn Alice McArthur that her life might be in danger.

When Rick Edgar got up the next morning, he grabbed the morning newspaper, to read about the homicide he had worked the day before. The McArthur murder was front-page news. Bold headlines demanded attention, and as Edgar smoked a cigarette, he settled into a chair to read what the reporters had to say.

"A small arrangement of flowers was found inside the home," according to Saturday's *Arkansas Democrat*. The *Arkansas Gazette* quoted the prosecutor as saying Alice apparently went to the front door to accept delivery of a floral plant.

That's sure strange, Edgar thought. He didn't see any flowers.

Edgar telephoned McNeely.

"What flowers are they talking about?" he asked. "Did you see any flowers?"

"No," McNeely answered.

On Monday morning the *Arkansas Gazette* reported: "A flower arrangement with a printed card which said, 'Have a nice day,' was found at Mrs.

McArthur's feet in the closet. The police have traced the arrangement, an assortment of a dozen flowers, to a Little Rock florist shop."

Edgar went back on duty Monday and saw McNeely.

"Did you see any flowers in the closet?" Edgar asked again.

"No," McNeely replied.

"Neither did I. I wouldn't have missed them. I touched her leg to feel the temperature, and I didn't see any flowers," Edgar said.

After talking with McNeely, Edgar made a point to take a look at the crime scene photos. Sure enough, there were the flowers, big as day, right at Alice's feet.

The original position of the bouquet of flowers became a topic of heated debate among law enforcement officers. Although crime scene photographs clearly show the flowers at Alice's feet, and although they were there by the time Detective Dawson arrived, both Edgar and McNeely stil maintain they did not see a bouquet of flowers when they checked Alice's body for signs of life. In addition, members of the sheriff's department later said they saw flower petals in the foyer of the home, which would support McClendon's claim that Alice dropped the flowers while running. But no flower petals show up in the police photographs of the foyer, and Dawson said he saw no petals. Dawson did, however, remember seeing the bouquet in the closet.

I got there around 6:00, and it was around midnight when I left. I went over every inch of that house, and I didn't find anything that looked like petals . . . we took pictures of every room on the upper floor and at varying angles. Nothing was moved, and nothing was disturbed, 8x10 color glossies, and they are good pictures, and there are no petals anywhere.

. . . Al Dawson, 1985

Chapter Thirteen

AFTER PHOEBE LEFT WORK ON JULY 2, SHE drove across the Arkansas River to North Little Rock and went to her husband's pawn shop. At about 5:15 p.m. she received a call from Orsini, who said she had just returned home from her appointment with McArthur.

"Bill told me the North Little Rock police have had a trap on my phone for a long time," Orsini said almost hysterically.

Phoebe couldn't understand why Orsini was so upset. She knew Orsini had asked the telephone company to place a trap on her phone, and she thought it was strange that Orsini would be in tears over an additional trap—even if it was placed without her knowledge.

"They're trying to blame me and Bill for all that's going on, Phoebe. My God! How many more people will have to be killed before they realize who is doing this?" Orsini was so upset Phoebe didn't know what to say.

"I would never do anything to hurt Bill, his children or his wife," Orsini said. "When are they going to leave us alone?"

Phoebe managed to interject a word of comfort or encouragement, and after awhile, Orsini calmed down. Suddenly, she said, "Hold on, Phoebe, there's someone at my door." When she got back to the phone she told Phoebe it was a black man, holding a box, but she didn't open the door.

"Oh, it's probably someone this time of the year wanting to mow your lawn, Lee. Look, I've got to go, Paul's closing the shop."

Phoebe hung up and didn't hear from Orsini again until later in the evening after Phoebe had learned of Alice's death. Orsini called her from the sheriff's office.

"What are you doing out there?" Phoebe asked.

"I called the sheriff's department because I was scared. This car kept coming around my house, driving back and forth, so I called them and when I described the car, they sent someone out to pick me up so I could give them a positive identification of the car. When the deputy got to my house and told me about Alice, he said a car like the one I saw had been seen in her neighborhood, too. I just couldn't believe it."

Phoebe began to feel very uncomfortable. "Just too many coincidences," she thought. She was frightened by what was happening, and she began to try to put the pieces together. Finally, she began to doubt some of what Orsini was telling her.

At about the same time, but miles away, McArthur sat in his living room. He didn't know how long he had sat there. His sense of time was lost somewhere within his subconscious where his mind was fighting against the urge to run out of the room and look for Alice. He sensed she was dead, even though no one had told him. But the last hour or so was blurred, and reality and dreams were all mixed up together.

The first person he realized was there was Assistant Little Rock Police Chief Doc Hale, who came into the room and said, "We're going to take Alice out of here, and we think you ought to go downstairs."

Now his conscious mind was grasping what was happening. With Hale's words came the realization that

Alice really was dead. He reached in his pocket for another cigarette and fumbled with it and his lighter until Hale reached over with a steady hand and held the lighter for him. He took a deep drag on the cigarette and felt dizzy. Hale placed his hand on McArthur's shoulder and led him toward the stairs.

McArthur went down into the den and sat on top of the pool table. Anita Prather was there. Someone called his parents. Mr. and Mrs. McArthur lived only a few miles away, and soon his mother, Billie, came to comfort him. Law enforcement officers were still there, but McArthur didn't pay any attention to them. His mother placed a call to Alice's family at Golden Meadow, but she started to cry and could not talk, and Hale had to take the telephone away from her. McArthur's father and uncle had already left town to get Robyn and Chuck from camp. The children would not be told why they were being summoned home. McArthur left instructions he would be the one to tell them. He felt it was his duty, and he wanted to be with them when they learned about their mother.

When the detectives finished inspecting the crime scene, they told McArthur they wanted him to come to the police station for questioning. About the same time, someone called from his aunt and uncle's house to say the children were back. McArthur's father and uncle had taken them to the uncle's home about a mile away from the McArthur home, and McArthur agreed to go to the police station after he talked to his children.

As he drove to his uncle's house, McArthur had no idea how he would tell Robyn and Chuck their mother was dead. He was pale, and lines in his face normally not noticeable made him look years older. When he saw his children he wanted to protect them and shield them from the hurt he knew they must face, but he knew he couldn't. Looking at Robyn was like looking at Alice; she had the same features and smooth, tan skin, the same athletic walk, and many of the same expressions. He knew he had to keep his own emotions under control. He had to be strong. That was the only way to pull Robyn and Chuck through this nightmare. So he took a deep breath and tried to smile, but they looked past the smile and into his eyes, and they knew something horrible had happened.

About an hour later McArthur's father drove him to the Little Rock Police Department. The questioning was very matter of fact. For now, all the police wanted to know was what McArthur did from the time he got home from work until the time Alice's body was found.

Phoebe went to bed late the night of July 2, after listening to news accounts of Alice's murder on both television and radio. Although the murder was a major news story, details of what actually happened were sketchy. She kept thinking about Alice and wondering why anyone would want to harm her. She remembered watching old murder mysteries on television when the solution to the crime was always overlooked because it was so simple. She wondered if this was the case of Alice's murder; maybe it was right in front of her, and she couldn't see it. By morning she was exhausted; she hadn't slept all night, and she was more confused than ever.

The next day the story of Alice's murder dominated the front pages of both daily newspapers, as it would for the months to come. Orsini called Phoebe at the pawn shop and said she needed to talk to her about something—it was urgent. She said she would be there in a few minutes. When Phoebe hung up, a sense of foreboding gripped her, and the hair on the back of her head seemed to be standing straight up. She was afraid, more afraid than she had ever been, and she suddenly realized that what frightened her most was Lee Orsini.

Over the next few days, Orsini called Phoebe continually. On Monday she told Phoebe she had gotten an anonymous phone call from a man who told her a black man named Larry McClendon was Alice's killer. She also said the caller told her that Forrest Parkman, a former Little Rock policeman who was a member of the Regional Organized Crime Information Center in Memphis, a federally funded non-profit organization, had put out a contract on three women: Orsini, Alice and Holly Troutt, Bob Troutt's ex-wife. The Information Center was an organization which sued Sheriff Robinson for $8.3 million for slander but settled out of court on the day Alice was killed. Robinson had been quoted in a local magazine as saying the ROCIC was a joke and that some of its members should be in jail. The ROCIC dropped the suit when Robinson agreed to pay an undisclosed sum of money.

Phoebe had very little contact with McArthur during the time between Alice's murder and funeral. The day before Alice's funeral, Orsini called Phoebe and asked if she could go to the funeral with her. Phoebe talked Orsini out of going by saying there would be a lot of publicity. Next, Orsini tried to find out if the body would be at the funeral home for friends and family to view. Orsini said she would go to the funeral home to see Alice, instead of to the funeral. Phoebe told her none of the friends of the family were going to the funeral home. In fact, the casket was to be closed to everyone except family.

On the day of Alice's funeral, Orsini again called Phoebe. This time she told her she had heard McArthur would be arrested as soon as the funeral was over. Orsini told Phoebe to get word to McArthur and warn him, but Phoebe told her she wasn't going to worry McArthur about something like that; he had enough on his mind already.

"I guess if he's an attorney, he can take care of himself, and I am not calling him."

"You've got to call him," Orsini pleaded.

"No!" Phoebe said.

On Wednesday, the day after the funeral, Chris Piazza, Pulaski County deputy prosecuting attorney, told Phoebe that Hall had implicated Orsini and she was a suspect. Piazza was surprised when Phoebe told him she and Orsini had become friends and talked to each other daily by telephone. He told her to stay in contact with Orsini and report back to him. Having her suspicions confirmed only made Phoebe feel more frightened. She had to pretend that everything was normal between them, all the while believing Orsini probably murdered Alice. That same day McArthur came back to the office for the first time since Alice's death. He had just come from the prosecuting attorney's office and had his brother-in-law, Leonard Miller, with him. Phoebe pulled him into her office and confronted him:

"Are you having an affair with Lee? We've always been honest with each other when the chips are down, and I have to know. Look me straight in the face and tell me if you did or you didn't."

"I did not," McArthur said.

"That's all I wanted to know," she said.

"Why?," he asked.

"Because she's always making these insinuations."

"Well, if you have anything to say, say it in front of Leonard. I don't want to stay in here where he can't hear."

"I don't have anything else to say, but Chris Piazza told me Lee's a suspect."

"He told me that too . . . I just can't understand, why her?"

Phoebe couldn't understand either, but she felt Piazza was right. Ever since that day at the pawn shop, she knew Orsini killed Alice, and she couldn't say how she knew. She just knew.

Bill didn't really talk about Lee being a suspect too much because it was just unbelieveable. I stayed in contact with him by talking to his mother. It was the next week before he came into the office, and we would just sit around. . . . We were there, but we were shells. Our minds were not there at all. We canceled his court for about a month, and he didn't see clients except for close friends. When I say we sat around a lot, we did.

Paranoia set in. Bill was afraid that he was going to die. He drew up a will . . . and he made me promise that if he was killed, and it was ruled a suicide, not to let that happen. I was to fight it, and he was worried about his children because we thought an attempt would be made on him.

He was so depressed, he wasn't really there because if he had been, he would have fought back. I wanted to have a press conference to tell his side, but he said just stay quiet. We knew what it was building up to, but we figured Dub Bentley could stop Tommy Robinson, and he couldn't.

. . . Phoebe Jones Pinkston, 1984

Chapter Fourteen

FORREST HAMILTON PARKMAN FIRST MET
Yankee Hall in 1974 when Parkman was a lieutenant in
charge of the Little Rock Police Department's Organized Crime and Intelligence Unit investigating an auto
theft ring in which Hall was involved.

Parkman was a student of more than forty law enforcement schools and courses during a career which
began in 1955 when he became a deputy sheriff in
Poinsett County, Arkansas. In 1961, he joined the
Forrest City Police Department as a patrolman, and a
year later he moved to Little Rock and joined the police department. At the LRPD his investigations into
organized crime in the area led to a tip that an under-
world contract had been put out to have him killed.
Parkman made a trip to New Orleans to ask the regional chief of organized crime for help in having the
contract canceled. The Mafioso leader, flanked by
bodyguards, was aloof and noncommittal during the
meeting, which was so stiff and formal it was more like
an audience with the Pope. He finally asked Parkman
why he had come to him.

"Because," the policeman quipped, "I'm out of
Goddamned dimes to pay the little nigger to start my
car every morning."

The don shook with laughter, and the ice was broken. He took Parkman aside and told him in a heavy

Italian accent not to worry: "That barking dog in Little Rock will not bite."

After Parkman's trip to New Orleans, the contract on his life was mysteriously canceled.

Parkman had a remarkable ability to remember even the smallest detail of an investigation, and he never forgot a face or a name. Those who worked with him knew him as someone who "lived and breathed" police work. He had contacts in law enforcement all over the nation and could call anywhere to get information. A man who could be comfortable with anyone, Parkman could smile a broad smile and talk in his slow Southern drawl and immediately earn people's trust and cooperation.

Parkman met with Yankee Hall in late May 1982 in an attempt to get information on some criminals working out of Hot Springs. Hall was evasive in his answers, and it became obvious to Parkman that Hall was trying to get information too, and Parkman wondered why.

Parkman didn't meet Hall again until after the McArthur murder. In the meantime, however, he heard on the streets that Hall was trying to get some dynamite and a silencer for a .38-caliber pistol. Parkman passed this information along to Mike Willingham, a young patrolman with the LRPD who had known Hall for many years. Parkman warned Willingham that Hall might try to use him to get information about investigations and warned him that Hall might be involved in some new criminal activity. Hall had worked in the garage owned by Willingham's father, and the two had become friends in spite of their different lifestyles. When Willingham asked Hall if it was true he was looking for a silencer and dynamite, Hall nodded.

"It's for some people from out of town," he said.

* * *

Parkman and his wife just returned from vacation on Saturday, July 3, and turned on the television when they heard the news about Alice McArthur. Parkman immediately called the LRPD and asked an officer if they had any leads yet. The officer told him they had just gotten a break in the case: A woman in a florist shop had given them a physical description of the man who purchased an arrangement of flowers just like the one found at Alice's feet. The officer read the description to Parkman.

"It fits Yankee to a tee," Parkman said. "That's going to be Yankee Hall."

The police sent a detective out to the florist shop with a photograph of Hall, but the photo was ten years old, and the woman could not identify Hall as the same man who purchased the flowers.

After learning about the woman's response, Parkman went to headquarters and looked at the photo: "I saw Yankee a month ago, and he doesn't look like this at all," he told the police.

The sheriff's office received an anonymous phone call that same day identifying Alice's killer as a black man named Larry Darnell McClendon.

On Sunday, the Fourth of July, Parkman went to visit a friend, Bill Williams, another former police officer, who now owned a computer store in Little Rock. During the conversation, Parkman's wife called to tell him that Willingham was trying to get in touch with him. He had called Parkman's home and told Parkman's wife it was urgent. He was waiting at a pay phone for Parkman to return his call.

When Parkman called, Willingham told him that Hall had been helping him move from his apartment and the two had been together on Saturday. He told him he had picked up Hall at his apartment about 1:30

p.m. Saturday and driven out Cantrell Road in the direction of Pleasant Valley. When they approached a flower shop and noticed a detective's car parked in front of the place, Hall became very nervous. Willingham said Hall asked him why the detective unit was there, and Willingham told him there had probably been a burglary at the shop. At that point, Hall said, "What if they got the guy that bought the flowers on that McArthur killing? They still wouldn't have enough to put a charge on him, would they?" Willingham told him that they would, and then Hall said, "Well, if they did convict him, would he get the death sentence, or could he tell what he knew and get life without parole?"

Willingham, realizing Hall might know something about the McArthur murder, told him that if he did know anything, he needed to talk to someone in the detective division of the LRPD. Hall said he had heard a few rumors but did not want to mention any names, and he refused to talk to a detective. Later on Saturday, Hall told Willingham he would take off for Mexico, rather than go back to the penitentiary for parole violation or anything else. Hall, on parole after pleading guilty in October 1979 to charges of cocaine possession and dealing, had been sentenced to five years in prison on each charge. The terms were to be served concurrently. He was sent to prison on November 13, 1979, and was paroled September 30, 1980.

"Lieutenant," Willingham said, "Yankee is still acting awfully funny, and he wants to talk to somebody because he's afraid they are going to revoke his parole. He's got to meet his parole officer Tuesday. He might come up with some more information on the McArthur murder, if you will talk to his parole people."

"Fine," Parkman said, "Bring him out to Bill Williams's place on Kavanaugh."

* * *

Hall arrived at Williams's place about 9 p.m. and again started playing a cat-and-mouse game with Parkman. He kept asking Parkman to go to the parole office with him on Tuesday and help him out.

"Well," Parkman said, "the hottest thing going, you can probably solve."

"What's that?"

"The McArthur case."

Hall shifted uneasily in his seat. "Well," he said, "everybody knows who had that done."

"Well, I don't. Tell me."

"Bob Troutt."

"How do you figure that?"

"Oh, Bob Troutt has been going with Alice McArthur for years."

"Well, do you know of anywhere they have been seen together?" Parkman asked.

"No, but I think I can find out."

"Good," Parkman said. "By the way, I think I know why you wanted dynamite."

"What do you mean?," Hall asked.

"Alice's car was blown up."

Hall never admitted anything, but he assured Parkman that he could find out who was responsible for Alice's death if Parkman would accompany him to see his parole officer and put in a good word for him.

Parkman remained noncommittal. When he began to press Hall on Alice's death, Hall said, "I'll tell you one thing, Mr. Forrest. If I had done it, I would not have done it the way they did."

"How's that?" Parkman said.

"Those flowers they left there."

"Yeah. What about them?"

"I would have gone to a cemetery and picked up the flowers. I wouldn't have went to a flower shop and bought them."

Parkman realized Yankee's remark was important. Although local newspapers had reported that Alice apparently opened her front door to receive a floral delivery, the papers had not reported that the floral arrangement had been purchased from a shop. A detective told Parkman this, however, and also told him about a card with the preprinted message, "Have a nice day," which was attached to the flower arrangement.

"You know, that's good thinking, Yankee."

"Yeah. That would have been the way I done it," Hall bragged. "I would have gone to a graveyard and got them and carried them up there."

"You know, Yankee, probably the dumb bastard that did it—he's probably half stupid enough, they will probably pick up his fingerprints off the card. He probably wore gloves, but you watch, he probably left at least one good print."

Parkman noticed Hall had begun to sweat, and he felt sure he had guessed right about the way Hall handled the card.

"The police would have checked that already if the prints had been on there," Hall said.

"No," Parkman said. "The lab's closed on weekends and holidays. But they'll come up with it. Wait and see."

When Hall left Parkman, Parkman called Little Rock police detectives and told them about his conversation with Hall. On the evening of Monday, July 5, two days after the sheriff's office received the anonymous call saying Larry McClendon killed Alice, the Little Rock police picked up Hall at his apartment and took him to headquarters for questioning. He did not resist, but he told the officers, "I'm not saying anything."

Doc Hale, who had known Hall for years because of Hall's frequent encounters with the law, went into the

The McArthur home at 24 Inverness Circle in Pleasant Valley.
(*Photo by Nyma Benner*, Arkansas Democrat)

Alice Miller McArthur in her wedding gown.

Alice and Bill McArthur at a birthday party for Bill.

The split foyer inside the McArthur home. *(LRPD Photo)*

A police photograph of the inside of the closet where Alice's body was found, and the deadly bouquet. *(LRPD Photo)*

Sheriff Tommy Robinson at a press conference. (*Photo by Nyma Benner,* Arkansas Democrat)

Eugene "Yankee" Hall, the ex-convict who confessed in return for a life sentence.
(*Photo by Nyma Benner,* Arkansas Democrat)

Bill McArthur, 1982.
(*Photo by Nyma Benner,* Arkansas Democrat)

Judge Randall Williams sits in a borrowed office in 1982.
(*Photo by Nyma Benner*, Arkansas Democrat)

Deputy Prosecutor Chris Piazza and Mary "Lee" Orsini at her trial in 1982.
(*Photo by Nyma Benner*, Arkansas Democrat)

Mary "Lee" Orsini during Bill McArthur's probable cause hearing. (*Photo by Nyma Benner*, Arkansas Democrat)

Larry McClendon looks toward family and friends as he is escorted from the Pulaski County Courthouse during his trial. (*Photo by Nyma Benner*, Arkansas Democrat)

Michael Swayze, right, and Marty Freeman, far left, under arrest. (*Photo by Clay Carson,* Arkansas Democrat)

Bill McArthur embraces his mother after the grand jury results were announced in 1983. His father looks on. (*Photo by Nyma Benner,* Arkansas Democrat)

interrogation room where Hall was placed and sat down. Hall immediately seemed at ease.

"Yankee, you've made the big number this time," Hale said. "You've got problems."

"Doc," Hall said, "I can give you the top and bottom of it if I can walk."

Hale stood up and looked at Hall and said, "No way. No way you're gonna walk."

Lee Orsini was at the sheriff's office on the night Doc Hale was interviewing Hall at police headquarters. Later that evening sheriff Tommy Robinson and Larry Dill left her at the sheriff's department and drove to Little Rock police headquarters to meet with Chief Sonny Simpson. While at the LRPD, Robinson and Dill learned that Doc Hale was looking for Orsini as a suspect in Alice's murder. Robinson had one of his deputies bring Orsini to the Little Rock Police Department for questioning.

When Orsini arrived, she had in her possession a tape which she had already played for Dill. She told the police she had taped the anonymous caller who told her Larry McClendon killed Mrs. McArthur. Hale showed her a Polaroid photograph of Hall, and she denied knowing him. The police did not have enough to hold her and released her, but Hale told his detectives to find the man whose voice was on the tape because only someone intimately familiar with the murder would know about McClendon.

Hall had been picked up for questioning Monday afternoon and about 3:30 a.m. Tuesday he was charged with capital felony murder. Flower shop employees identified Hall in a police lineup as the man who had purchased the flowers found at the crime scene. Two of Hall's prints matched those on the flower arrangement, one on the card and one on the small container which held the carnations and daisies. Shortly after his arrest, Hall identified McClendon as the killer and implicated Orsini, and the police believed they had enough information to arrest McClendon on probable cause before he had a chance to flee. Later that morning, as the McArthur children were preparing for their mother's funeral, the police picked up McClendon, and later in the day they impounded his car, a 1970 Cadillac De Ville with a brown roof and gold body.

Hall's attorneys, Paul Johnson and David Williams, and the prosecutor's office began negotiating for Hall's confession. In the meantime, Doc Hale intensified his search for the person who made the anonymous phone call to Orsini. Hale knew that person held the key to solving the crime.

McArthur had already answered questions from Hale and the detectives of the Homicide Division of the Little Rock Police Department, but he had to go to police headquarters the afternoon of Alice's funeral to answer more. Shortly before leaving his parents' Little Rock home, he received news that a suspect had been arrested. Recalling these events later, he said he felt emotionally drained after the funeral, but the news of an arrest sent a wave of expectation through him. He was anxious to learn the details and find some explanation for what had happened to Alice. It was not knowing that drove him crazy when he finally closed his eyes at night—that and reliving the horror in his mind of Alice being pursued through their home.

Most of the policemen knew McArthur, and he knew that if anyone could solve this case, it was Doc Hale. The day Alice was killed, Hale told him, "Bill, we're going to make this one. There's too much evidence left around. I promise, we're going to solve it."

McArthur greeted Hale and the other officers as he entered the interrogation room. His presence there this time was a strange reversal of circumstances—he had faced most of them in the courtroom at one time or another. As he settled himself into a chair and the questioning began, he detected a change in the way Hale looked at him. Something in Hale's voice made McArthur feel uneasy.

It finally hit him. The police suspected him. Hale told him the suspect they had arrested that morning, Yankee Hall, had given a statement implicating McArthur and Mary Lee Orsini. Although Hall said he never met McArthur, he told police that Orsini assured him McArthur commissioned the killing.

McArthur was afraid if Alice's family returned to Louisiana and heard this allegation from someone else, they might believe it. "I've got to get someone here to hear this face to face," he thought.

Alice's family was getting ready to leave for the airport when McArthur reached them at their motel and asked to speak to his brother-in-law, Leonard Miller.

"Leonard, you've got to stay. Let the rest of them go home, but you've got to come down here to the police station. There's something you have to hear."

Miller was solemn when he entered the interrogation room and greeted his brother-in-law. McArthur's face showed signs of stress, and his cheeks were beginning to take on a slightly hollow appearance.

As Hale told Miller about Hall's statement, Miller sat stoically, never looking at McArthur, never changing his expression. When Hale finished, Miller looked at McArthur and asked, "Is there any truth to it?"

"Not a bit," McArthur answered.

"I would hate for my sister to be killed over something like that," Miller said. Then he looked at Hale and said, "I don't believe it."

McArthur was relieved. It was important to him that his brother-in-law believe him, but now he was thinking of his children. It was more important that they believe him.

As they left the police station, Miller turned to McArthur, "I don't know about you, but I need a drink."

The two men went to a bar near the police headquarters where they ordered one drink after another. They drank in silence. McArthur was grateful Miller didn't question him. He felt all his emotions were used up. His brain had slowed down, and his thought processes were shutting down, allowing the alcohol to do its job.

Finally, after their third or fourth drink, Miller smashed the butt of his cigarette in the ashtray on the bar, turned toward McArthur and said, "Brother-in-law, get ready because they are going to give you unmitigated hell."

The Seasons said their special goodbye to Alice after the funeral. They met at Alice's grave. Tom Brewer brought iced champagne: Korbel, only the best for Alice. Someone remembered the Vantage cigarettes, Alice's brand. And another member of the group furnished champagne glasses.

They prayed. They sang Alice's favorite songs. They toasted Alice in death to honor her life and the joy she had brought to each of them. When they were through, they smashed Alice's champagne glass and buried the broken pieces along with a Vantage cigarette on top of her grave, just underneath the freshly disturbed soil.

When a cemetery worker noticed some of the broken glass and a couple of champagne bottles the Seasons left behind, he called the police. Once the news media reported the incident, rumors circulated that McArthur and a woman everyone suspected was Orsini had toasted his wife's death.

A few months later, long after Alice's friends had explained they had not "frolicked" on her grave, but simply toasted Alice's memory, a crime magazine sensationalized the slaying and the champagne episode this way:

"Beside the murdered woman's grave lay two empty

champagne bottles and a couple of empty glasses. It looked like whoever killed her drank a toast to her death and danced on her grave...."

Bill McArthur is not the kind of man who would kill the mother of his children. I know Bill. I have always found him to be a man of integrity. That means so much to your character, that it is basically how you are, and I don't believe people can change that much from their own personality.... I didn't consider him to be a suspect.

....Jess F. "Doc" Hale, 1987

Chapter Fifteen

WILLIAM LARRY BURGE, A SHERWOOD RE-
altor, first met Lee Orsini after her husband was murdered. Burge came by her house to talk to her about
selling it. She impressed him as being timid, frightened
of something unknown, fearful that whoever killed her
husband might come back and kill her. He believed
she needed help, and both Burge and his wife became
friends with her.

One afternoon after she had canceled an open house
for some prospective buyers, Burge stopped by the
house to talk to her, and she told him she canceled it
because an anonymous caller said there was a bomb
planted in the middle of her house. Soon afterward,
about April 14, 1982, she told Burge someone with a
Cajun accent had called and threatened her.

Burge and Orsini's friendship eventually developed
to a point where she gave him a key to her house. She
borrowed his car often, and he stopped by frequently.
She began to rely on Burge for advice, comfort and
protection. She told him Bill Younts, the chief of police in North Little Rock, was involved in organized
crime. She wanted Burge to write a letter to the *Arkansas Democrat* and say that he had overheard a conversation between Younts and another individual and
quote Younts as saying, "If I thought I could get away
with it, I would kill that Orsini bitch."

Burge refused to write the letter. He told her it just
wasn't right. She called Burge later and apologized for

asking him to write the letter, and she explained she was angry when she made the request and didn't mean what she said.

One morning she picked Burge up in Dr. Charles Wulz's Cadillac, and the two drove to a beautiful little lake within the Lakewood area of North Little Rock. Burge couldn't help but notice several guns in the car, but he pretended nothing was unusual. A few minutes after she parked near the lake, a police car drove by and she grabbed for one of the guns, convincing Burge she was truly frightened of the police.

Orsini always compared Burge to McArthur and told Burge they both were the kind of men she was attracted to. She also told Burge that McArthur had asked her if she would go out with him if he wasn't married, and she said she would.

Burge had several friends at the North Little Rock Police Department. One of them learned he had been seen at her house and warned him to stay away from her because she was a suspect in her husband's murder and was dating a thug named Yankee Hall. Burge didn't believe she had anything to do with Ron's death, but he confronted her about Hall on May 14. She told him she didn't know anybody by that name.

A couple of days after Alice's murder, Orsini called Burge and told him she had received another anonymous telephone call. This time the caller told her who killed Alice McArthur, and she wanted to get the information to Sheriff Robinson, but she didn't want to get involved and wind up with her name in the newspapers again, she said.

"Let's just make an anonymous call and tape it. Then we can give the tape to the sheriff," she told Burge.

Burge agreed to help her. He went to her house, and she provided him with notes she had written on yellow legal paper. He went to a nearby telephone booth and

called her and read from the notes which identified
McClendon as the killer.

On Tuesday, July 6 at 6 a.m., Burge awoke to the
ringing of his telephone. He rubbed his eyes and
picked up the receiver.

"Larry," he heard Orsini say, "You are not going to
believe who they've arrested," she said.

Burge was still half asleep, but he came wide awake
when he heard the name, "Yankee Hall."

She told Burge she now remembered a man named
"Hall" had done some body work on her car.

"You don't think he could be the same one, do
you?" she asked innocently.

As early as May, when Alice's car was bombed, Sheriff
Robinson told the news media he wondered whether
the Troutt and Orsini cases resulted from a movement
in organized crime to take over Arkansas, and he
mentioned the possibility that narcotics, pornography
and prostitution might be involved. Shortly after Alice
was killed, the sheriff said he thought her murder and
the Ron Orsini murder were related. These types of
statements together with news reports that contained
small factual errors and innuendo, resulted in a perception by many people that Bill McArthur was involved in his wife's slaying. For example, the day after
the murder the *Arkansas Democrat* reported
McArthur "summoned" Anita Prather to his home,
and that he was searching the yard when she found the
body. On Monday the *Democrat* reported McArthur
left his home when he found the front door open and
went to the Prather home to telephone police. Also on
Monday, the *Arkansas Gazette* published a story about
Alice's oil lease inheritance, saying that "area law enforcement officials are exploring the possibility that
the inheritance constitutes part of the motive." The
report raised questions about who Alice's beneficiaries
were and said she had talked about putting the money

in trust for her children shortly after her car was bombed. Elaborating further and thus casting more suspicion on McArthur, the *Arkansas Gazette* reported, "Although friends said she was certain in her own mind that the bomb was meant for her, it could not be learned whether she carried through with the trust or even left a will." Then on Wednesday the *Arkansas Gazette* said additional arrests were expected, and the *Arkansas Democrat* reported that Robinson told someone the sheriff's office had "tapped the McArthur phone since the bombing." The next day, July 8, the *Arkansas Gazette* allowed Orsini to link McArthur directly to his wife's murder by reporting statements she made during an interview with the newspaper. The article said Orsini confirmed she had been questioned by the Little Rock police and was told, "she was suspected of having conspired with McArthur, who is her attorney, to have his wife killed." A few days later the *Arkansas Democrat* learned of the $25,000 mortgage Orsini had given McArthur, and the *Arkansas Gazette* reported the McArthur probe was widening in a headline which read, "Orsini linked to club owned by victim's husband." On Monday, July 12, the *Arkansas Democrat* managing editor John Robert Starr referred to the *Arkansas Gazette* story of July 8, and without naming McArthur, Starr pointed out that the *Arkansas Gazette* allowed Mrs. Orsini to link someone to the crime on her unsupported word. Starr summed up the situation when he wrote, "There has been some extremely irresponsible reporting on this investigation. Some of it has been libelous if certain persons are not subsequently charged."

Meanwhile, the Little Rock police were busy trying to find out the identity of the man on the tape recording Orsini had given the sheriff. Although they were out of their jurisdiction in North Little Rock, they watched her house and took down the license numbers of vehicles parked there. One of the automobiles they checked was registered to William Larry Burge.

On Friday morning, July 16, Detective Dawson called Burge and asked him to come down to the police station for questioning about the tape. Burge was beginning to get a bad feeling about Orsini as he drove south over the Arkansas River bridge toward the Little Rock police station. When he arrived, Dawson and Detective Fred Hensley played the tape and asked him if he was the man on the tape recording. Burge did not admit it was his voice, but Dawson and Hensley knew it was. When they told him the anonymous caller could be charged in connection with Alice's murder, Burge's face reddened, he started to say something but stopped. Hensley thought Burge looked terribly worried.

"You let me go, and I'll go get her, and we'll get this shit straightened out," Burge said.

"Okay," Hensley agreed. "But don't make us have to come looking for you."

Burge called Orsini before he left the police station and said he needed to talk to her right away. They agreed that Burge would pick her up at Wulz's house, but when he arrived at the house, Orsini wasn't there so he went to Wulz's office. The receptionist told him that Wulz and Orsini were having lunch at a nearby restaurant. When Burge arrived at the restaurant, Wulz was seated at a table. Burge joined him, and they both waited for Orsini to come out of the ladies' room. When she approached the table, she motioned for Burge to get up so they could talk privately. Burge begged her to come with him to the police station to straighten things out, but she refused even after he told her he thought he was going to be arrested. Wulz got up to leave, and Burge volunteered to drive Orsini home. He thought that would give him a little more time to talk her into going to the police with him.

During the drive Burge kept trying to get her to change her mind:

"I'm going to go tell the truth, Lee. It's truth time."

"No, don't you let them run you around, go put it on them. You're the best I've ever seen, you can handle them."

"It's not a matter of handling them, Lee. It's a matter of telling it like it is, and I am damn sure not going to be involved in complicity to murder."

As he parked the car in front of Wulz's house, Orsini fumbled around inside her purse for the housekeys. Burge became frightened as his mind began going over the events of the past week. The fact that she would not go to the police with him made him realize she had been lying to him. Fearing she might have a gun in her purse, he stepped out of the car and backed away from it, trying not to allow his fear to show.

"I'll go check your car and see if they're in there," he said, keeping his eyes on Orsini.

After a few more seconds, she said, "Oh, here they are," and got out of the car, holding a set of keys in her hand.

He practically ran back to the car and left, headed for his attorney's office.

Burge returned to the police station with his lawyer, and after he was guaranteed immunity from prosecution, he admitted he had made the so-called anonymous telephone call to Orsini's residence, but he said the whole thing had been her idea. He told them she even made notes on yellow legal paper for him to refer to when making the call, and he turned over the notes to the police.

After getting Burge's statement on Friday afternoon, July 16—two weeks after Alice McArthur's murder—Little Rock police arrested Orsini about 6:30 p.m. at her mother's apartment. Detective Dawson advised Orsini she was under arrest for capital murder for the death of Alice McArthur and advised her of her rights. She was then taken to the LRPD by Dawson, Hensley and another detective, and when they searched her purse for weapons, they found a five-shot derringer.

At 9:10 p.m. the officers brought Orsini out of the detective division, past waiting reporters, to the jail. She requested the police not take her jewelry until she got past the television cameras.

Three days later Orsini pleaded innocent in municipal court to the capital murder charge. She was remanded to the Pulaski County Jail under the custody of the sheriff's department and held without bond. Bond had already been denied both Hall and McClendon, who were also being held in the county jail. In Arkansas a person can be arraigned in municipal court, but municipal court has no authority to handle felony cases. Since all three defendants would be tried in circuit court, the county sheriff retains custody of felony defendants until trial. A few days after Orsini's plea and arraignment, a circuit court judge set an October 4 trial date in her case. At the same time, a request for bond for Orsini was again denied because Prosecuting Attorney Bentley objected due to the seriousness of the charge and complexity of the case. A bond hearing was set for Orsini a few days later, but Sheriff Robinson said if she were released on bond, he would immediately arrest her on another charge to keep her in the Pulaski County Jail. Bond was denied Orsini a third time on Tuesday, July 27, eleven days after her arrest, when Deputy Prosecutor Chris Piazza said he feared that if she were released on bond, she would be a great risk to her friends and other members of the community.

Soon after Orsini's arrival at the county jail, rumors began trickling out that she was receiving special treatment.

* * *

She could get upset, she could cry in a minute, she could just go to pieces for you, and she did on the tape we made that day, and that scared me and got me to thinking because she could turn it on and off so quickly.

. . . Larry Burge, 1984

Chapter Sixteen

AFTER LEE ORSINI'S ARREST, SHERIFF ROBinson began criticizing the LRPD and the prosecutor's handling of the investigation and claiming there was some sort of coverup going on, and he said despite the arrests, he was not going to stop working on the case. The sheriff told reporters he was "sick of people screwing up the case," and he said his office would not share its information on the case with anyone. A few days later Prosecutor Bentley subpoenaed Robinson's files on the case because Robinson had refused to turn them over willingly. Robinson finally relinquished his files to Bentley on July 26, but less than a week later, Robinson renewed his criticism of Bentley, saying the prosecutor wasn't trying to get convictions in the McArthur case. He also said the LRPD had coordinated their investigation with Bentley and prematurely arrested Orsini. The sheriff said he had planned to follow her out of town on July 19, but "the dumb butts arrested her." Robinson's mounting criticism created bad feelings between his agency and the LRPD which completely eroded the spirit of cooperation that had existed in the past and caused the rank and file officers of each agency to distrust those of the other.

At Lee Orsini's bond hearing on July 27 it was revealed that a pistol belonging to Dr. Charles Wulz had been missing since the first of July. Also missing were five .38-caliber custom-made shells for the pistol. On

July 28, Prosecutor Bentley told reporters he would seek the death penalty for Orsini, McClendon and Hall.

Robinson's criticism of Bentley gained momentum each day and became the center of attention of the news media. He said he would try to have Bentley disqualified from trying the cases. He claimed the prosecutor was trying to silence state witnesses: "He's afraid of what they might say," Robinson said.

August started off with more open hostility between Robinson and Bentley. Bentley told the media if Robinson "were half the cop he claims to be, Alice McArthur might be alive today." Bentley said he believed the sheriff could have prevented Alice's murder because someone had told Robinson the day after the bombing incident that there was an "association" between Orsini and Hall. Bentley also said the sheriff had undertaken the responsibility of providing protection for Alice and had on several occasions stationed deputies at the McArthur residence. "I assume," Bentley said, "that he didn't have anybody there at the time of her murder."

A few days later Robinson revealed he had secretly taped some telephone conversations with Bentley to prove the prosecutor had botched the McArthur case. He said he would file a libel suit against the prosecutor and release the tape-recordings to the public unless Bentley apologized, and he again claimed Bentley did not want to get to the bottom of the McArthur case.

Throughout the month of August, the open warfare between Bentley and Robinson hogged the headlines. A circuit court judge who imposed a gag order in the case said he was disturbed by the "totally unprofessional conduct" of both Robinson and Bentley. On the day the gag order was issued, Robinson called a local newspaper to question whether the judge could "order me not to speak out against what I perceive as a travesty in reference to the McArthur case." On August 25 Robinson said there was one more suspect in the slaying. On

August 27 Robinson told the news media, "I'm tired of playing games with mealy-mouthed people. I'm going to find out what happened. I am going to turn this town upside down until I get to the bottom of this." Two days later he told a meeting of the Arkansas Associated Press Broadcasters' Association that he was trying to get the prosecuting attorney to give him some records in the case, and if Bentley did not provide them, "You're going to see some heads roll."

The battle between Bentley and Robinson, and the resultant media madness, prompted the following editorial in the Springdale, Arkansas, newspaper:

> Wilbur 'Dub' Bentley and Tommy Robinson, the Laurel and Hardy for law enforcement, have it straight from a judge. Do any more talking about the McArthur murder case and you're going to wish you hadn't.
>
> These two must be driving Lady Justice crazy, constantly yelling in her ear, as blindfolded, she tries to balance the scales of fairness in a sensational Little Rock murder case. Frankly, we think the Little Rock media, in its competitive zeal, has ridiculously overplayed the murder. . . .
>
> But the media has had plenty of help from Talking Tall Tommy Robinson, the Pulaski County sheriff, and his seemingly willing foil, Prosecutor 'Dub' Bentley. . . .
>
> If we appear to be taking more than a passing interest in a far away murder case, it's for two reasons. First, Tommy Robinson, who once was director of the state Department of Public Safety, obviously has bigger political aspirations than sheriff, and we're just hearing from him.
>
> Second, this 'high society' murder has thrown the Little Rock media into a tizzy and made a mockery of justice. The case is a classic example of everything the media and law enforcement officers should not do in handling pretrial publicity.
>
> If Lady Justice manages to struggle through this one

without being knocked down in the scuffle between
Robinson and Bentley, it will be her finest hour.

Although Hall had already confessed to the Little
Rock police, on Sunday, August 29, he gave the prosecutor a formal, sworn statement alleging Mary "Lee"
Orsini had arranged Alice's slaying. He made the
statements as part of a plea bargain arrangement allowing him to plead guilty and receive a life sentence.
In his statement, Hall said Orsini told him McArthur
wanted his wife dead because she was going to leave
him, ruin his law practice, and take the children.

The last Sunday afternoon in August was the kind of
scorcher that makes time creep, miserably and sweat-
ily, painfully drawing summer to a close. The water in
the McArthurs' pool was more like a lukewarm bath
than a refreshing place to hide from the sun. McArthur
and his two children lazed by the pool, trying to exert
as little effort as possible. They cooked hamburgers on
the grill and watched the hot, dry day drag by.

McArthur suspected the sheriff's next move, and he
wanted to prepare Robyn and Chuck for it. After dinner he told them he thought he would soon be arrested, and not let it bother them because he would
only be in jail for a little while, and he would prove his
innocence in the long run.

They expressed surprise and fear that their father,
too, would be taken away from them. But he reassured
them and told them no matter what was said about him
in the newspapers or on television, no matter what the
sheriff said about him, it wasn't true, and he promised
them he would not be taken away from them very long.
They tried to make him feel better by putting on a brave
front, but both were terrified at the thought of their
father being in jail. Their concern for their father had
evidenced itself since their mother's death in an almost
parental protectiveness toward him. They were careful
not to talk about their mother much in his presence, and

they tried to cheer him up when he seemed depressed. The three of them were closer than ever before.

About 5 p.m. the next day, Captain Bobby Woodward walked into McArthur's office. Phoebe looked up from her typing and the smile with which she had prepared to greet their visitor froze on her face when she saw who it was. She noticed Woodward's belt buckle, which was shaped like a western-style six-shooter, and she tried to ease the tension of the moment by joking about it.

"Hey, Bobby, what's that on your belt? You gonna shoot someone?"

"Yeah," Woodward replied, laughing self-consciously.

McArthur came out of his office, and Phoebe saw the color drain from his face. Although he was trying to act calm, Phoebe knew he was scared, and she tried to give him a little moral support, if not in words, in the way she looked at him. She would stand behind him, even if nobody else did.

"The sheriff wants to talk to you, Bill," Woodward said.

"Well, is it all right if I drive my own car out there?"

"Sure, I don't see why not," Woodward said. McArthur knew he was going to be arrested. Phoebe knew it, too. He called his attorney, Jack Holt, Jr. Holt agreed to meet him at the sheriff's department, but he said it would be at least an hour before he could get there.

McArthur drove his own car, followed by Woodward. His law partner, Jack Lassiter, followed about fifteen minutes later.

When he arrived at the sheriff's department, reporters were already there. Someone had tipped them off about the arrest.

McArthur was taken into an office where Major Larry Dill and Tom Waggoner, a deputy, were waiting for him:

"We want to talk to you," Dill said.

"Fine. Are you going to advise me of my rights and ask me questions?"

"Yes."

"In that case, I'll wait for Jack Holt to get here. He's on his way, and when he gets here, I'll answer any questions you have."

The three men sat in silence for a few minutes, then the telephone on Dill's desk rang. It was getting close to 6 o'clock news time, and McArthur suspected the party on the other end of the line was Robinson.

"Yes, he's here. He says he'll answer our questions, but we're waiting for Jack Holt to get here," Dill said.

McArthur could tell from Dill's reaction that Robinson told him to go ahead and make the arrest. Dill hung up and started filling out an arrest report.

Neither Dill nor Waggoner would look at him, so McArthur asked, "Are you getting ready to arrest me?"

"Yeah," Dill answered.

"Both of you know this is a bunch of bullshit," McArthur said. "This is wrong, both of you know that."

McArthur was arrested that evening—Monday, August 30—for conspiracy to commit capital murder based upon probable cause, without a warrant. After the formal arrest was made, McArthur was taken down the hall and through the main lobby past a crowd of photographers and reporters. When Holt arrived, he told McArthur they could probably get a judge to post bond so he would not have to spend the night in jail, but McArthur said he would rather wait because he didn't want it to appear he was receiving special treatment.

Dill gave Holt a list of questions which Holt showed McArthur. He agreed to answer them provided the other agencies involved in investigation of the case were present, such as the federal Bureau of Alcohol, Tobacco and Firearms, the Little Rock and North Little Rock Police Department, and the prosecuting attorney's office. But the questions were not asked that night nor the next day nor the next. However, Robinson and Dill told the media that McArthur had refused to answer a list of questions put to him by the sheriff and that was why the sheriff arrested him.

About 10 p.m., after changing into jail garb, a glo-orange jumpsuit and tennis shoes, McArthur was ushered into a private cell. He didn't see any other prisoners because his cell was apart from the others. He refused to eat the meal one of the jailers brought. Instead, he lay on his cot and tried to sleep. Eventually he did, for during the night strange faces and distorted images popped into his head, muddling the events of the past few weeks into a nightmare.

The next morning a story in the *Arkansas Democrat* reported McArthur's arrest:

> Sheriff Tommy Robinson said he had received a lot of 'pressure to back off' from arresting McArthur, but 'I had to do in my heart what was right.'
>
> 'I'm taking a real chance,' the sheriff said. 'Not everybody in the criminal justice system is in agreement with me.'
>
> .. Dill has been spearheading the sheriff's office investigation of the slaying and had a list of eighteen questions to ask McArthur, who was charged after refusing to make any statement.
>
> Robinson would not elaborate on the list other than to say they were 'pretty hard-nosed questions.' He noted that he was still under a court gag order not to publicly discuss details of the investigation.
>
> 'We made up our mind today that if he [McArthur] didn't answer the questions, we'd make an arrest based on statements from Yankee Hall and other corroborating evidence,' Robinson said. The sheriff wouldn't say what other evidence he had.

The story went on to explain a few other details of the

arrest and continued quoting Robinson, who said he had felt all along that McArthur was involved in the slaying.

It also reported that Jack Holt, McArthur's attorney, explained that McArthur had not refused to answer Dill's questions but had insisted the prosecuting attorney, Little Rock police investigators and FBI agents be present to hear his answers.

The *Arkansas Gazette* quoted Robinson as saying he felt his evidence against McArthur "is just as strong at this point as the evidence" he had against McClendon and Orsini. The *Gazette* story also reported that Holt had insisted McArthur never declined to give a statement.

The next morning McArthur entered an innocent plea, and Pulaski County Municipal Judge David Hale released him on a $50,000 recognizance bond. The same day, Dub Bentley withdrew from prosecuting the charge against McArthur and recommended Wayne Matthews of Pine Bluff, Arkansas, as special prosecutor. Robinson objected to Matthews's appointment because Matthews, who was prosecuting attorney of the Eleventh Judicial District, had clashed with Robinson in 1978 while Robinson was state public safety director.

Judge Hale took Bentley's suggestion of a special prosecutor under consideration and eventually offered the job to the prosecutor from the First Judicial District, Gene Raff of Helena, Arkansas. After spending a week and a half reviewing the case, Raff turned it down, saying he didn't have the time to prosecute it. But Raff later told a friend he turned it down because there wasn't enough evidence to warrant prosecution of McArthur.

Hale then asked former United States Attorney W.H. "Sonny" Dillahunty of Little Rock to serve as special prosecutor on the charge against McArthur of conspiracy to commit capital murder. Dillahunty accepted the appointment.

Although McArthur was released on the recognizance bond August 31, a hearing to determine whether

the sheriff had probable cause to arrest him was not
held until November. The delay occurred because all
six Pulaski County circuit judges recused themselves
from the case and another judge had to be found to
preside over the hearing. When the hearing was finally
held, it was the longest in the state's history.

On Thursday morning, September 2, 1982, the two
statewide daily newspapers carried stories about Hall's
sworn confession. The McArthur murder had become
one of the biggest continuing news stories of the de-
cade. The *Arkansas Gazette* reported the content of
Hall's confession, and the *Arkansas Democrat* obtained a copy of the confession from an unidentified
source and printed it almost in its entirety. Nonrele-
vant material and names were omitted.

Newspaper boxes sold out as people rushed to get
their personal copies of Hall's confession and read
what he had to say about McArthur's involvement in
his wife's slaying.

*I don't believe I was ever misquoted in the newspapers,
at least not significantly, but I watched and read things
with impunity. They printed things that with the slightest
bit of investigation, they could have found out were
without merit, but they were allowed to print them without fear of being hurt because they had a 'source,' gen-
erally being the sheriff's office, and they printed things
that were totally baseless. . . .*

. . . William C. "Bill" McArthur, 1984

Chapter Seventeen

YANKEE HALL'S SWORN CONFESSION WAS made to Chris Piazza, a deputy prosecuting attorney for Pulaski County, about 6 p.m., on Sunday, August 29, 1982 at the Pulaski County jail, the day before McArthur's arrest. Those present included Robinson, Dill and Hall's attorney, Paul Johnson.

A tape-recorder was turned on and Hall was advised of his rights. His attorney stated for the record the conditions under which Hall would make the statement: that the prosecutor would recommend to the court that Hall be allowed to plead guilty and receive a sentence of life and that Hall be "ready, willing and able to testify to those statements should he ever be subpoenaed to court."

". . . She told me the reason he wanted to do this was, evidently Mrs. McArthur was planning on leaving Bill McArthur, this is what she told me now, you know, take his kids and she was talking about just wiping out his law practice," Hall said. "I don't know what she knew on him, but she indicated that he knew or she knew something that would just bury his practice, and she was going to take his nightclub and just everything away from him, you know, and which I didn't care about the reason, and she kept telling me all that stuff."

Hall told them how he and Orsini planted the bomb in Alice's car and about an earlier attempt at planting the bomb that failed. He said he got some explosives from a man named Carl Wilson and took them to Orsini's house, where he made the bomb. He said he and Orsini made several trips to the McArthur neighborhood, "Because she wasn't even sure what kind of car belonged to Mrs. McArthur."

One night, Hall and Orsini pretended to be joggers and jogged up and down the street in front of the McArthur home. Orsini sneaked over to the McArthur driveway and verified that the beige Cutlass belonged to Mrs. McArthur, he said. And once when he and Orsini went to the McArthur home to put the bomb on the car, they discovered Mrs. McArthur's car was in the garage, so they had to disarm the bomb and try again later. He said Orsini told him she would make sure that Mrs. McArthur's car was left out the next time.

"And then after that, she informed me the nights that the car would be out . . . she always knew when the car was going to be out ahead of time, you know, and when it was going to be in," Hall said.

Hall said that the night he put the bomb on Alice's car, May 20, Orsini was with him. The next morning, he called Orsini, and she already knew what had happened, although news of the incident had not yet been on television or radio:

"She [Lee] knew that the bomb had partially detonated and when I called her, in fact, I says, 'What's happening?,' you know, I had just gotten up, you know, and she said, 'Well, let me tell you what's happened.' She was kind of sarcastic, you know, kind of disgusted.

"She says, 'Bill just called me' and she said, 'he informed me that he just got a call from his wife and she informed him that she pulled out of her driveway, and a bomb went off underneath her car and blew a hole in the floor, and she had her legs scratched up a bit, but she wasn't hurt bad.'

"And she said he was on his way to comfort his wife,

you know, and I just didn't know what happened, I was just kind of dumbfounded, you know, and of course we all just stayed low for a while and didn't really talk about it for a few days.

"And then she came back and said, 'Well,' she says, 'He still wants something done,' you know, I said, 'Well, I don't know, it's gonna be bad,' you know, and then she come up with more money.

"She said, 'Well,' she says, 'If we could do it,' she says, 'he'll pay $20,000 if we can still do it,' you know."

Hall continued telling about hiring McClendon as the "hit man" and how Orsini furnished a gun she had stolen from Dr. Charles Wulz to be used as the murder weapon, a .38-caliber Smith and Wesson. He said he asked her about the McArthur children and she said she mentioned it to McArthur, who told her that the children were going to camp the following week.

Hall said: "... but it had to be done that week bcause they would be back the following Monday, just turned out to be the Fourth of July weekend coming up.

"Well, we had a little trouble all week, I forgot just what happened—we never did get it done until Friday of the second and we even had trouble that day getting out there, we didn't get there til real late, and I had picked up the sign she made and the clipboard and the gun. I didn't already have them, you know; in fact, I left the sign and clipboard in this Corvette that I was driving because the darn motor blew up in it, and we had to drive over to North Little Rock to pick up the sign and the clipboard that day, you know, and we drove back to the apartment where I had the gun and the bullets that she had furnished and Mrs. McArthur wasn't home.

"I had called several times, and she wasn't home, ... me and Larry had just give up on it around lunch time and he went on home—and I called Lee about 2:30 in the afternoon and she informed me that Mrs.

McArthur was home now, and I told her I didn't know if we had time to get it done before Bill got home, you know, and she said that she was in touch with Bill, and that he was waiting to hear from her, and she would hold him up til we were done.

"In fact, she said that they were going out of town for the weekend, and he was expected home early, so for us to get right on it, you know.

"And I called Larry back, and he come over to the house, and we decided we had to use his car, and it had a burned wire . . . and the car wouldn't start. We were just having more problems, so I run out here, and I found the trouble on his car, and while he was replacing the wire, I showed him how to repair the wire, I went and borrowed some jumper cables, and I came back and I was in . . . Mike Willingham's truck, you know, and I pulled up there, and we were charging his battery, his battery had run down, and Lee drove by while we were doing this, in front of my apartment, and I guess she was wondering if we were going to get it done or not, and I motioned to her that, everything was okay, we were just having a little problem with the car. . . . And she nodded and took off.

"She informed me that Bill had set up an appointment for her that afternoon so she would have a good alibi, and she could state that she was at her attorney's office when this happened, you know, she was going to be over there so there wouldn't be any doubt about her alibi, and I take it she was on her way to the attorney's office then. She nodded and waved, and she departed, and we finally got Larry's car started, and all we liked [lacked] then was the flowers that we were going to use to act like a delivery, and we started out Highway 10.

"I was in the pickup, and Larry was in his car and then I remembered we left the apartment door open cause we were in a hurry, it was getting awful late, it was already, I think, about 3:30, and I pulled over by

the Miller Tire Co. . . . And I informed Larry that we
left the darn apartment door open at my place, so he
said he'd go back and shut it and lock it, and I went to
the florist, and then I drove out on the west side of
[Interstate] 430 on Cantrell, and I pulled off the
shoulder . . . and I waited for Larry to come by, and
when he came by I just put everything in his car, and
we drove to the McArthur residence.

"First we pulled over in the church parking lot and
took the license tag off of his car and placed this sign
that Lee had made in the window, and since Larry was
going to go in and take care of everything—I was driving, and he was getting ready, he was checking the gun
and getting ready to go in there—and we drive by, and
there was people out in the yard, and we didn't know
if it was a good time or not, you know. And then we
figured out there'd always be somebody out there on a
nice day, so we just backed in the driveway, and I told
Larry that for sure not to leave anything, and I said,
'In fact, once you go in, I'll kind of get out of the car,
and when I hear. . . .' you know, I could hear the shots,
when I heard that everything was going to be all right,
I was going to go in and make . . . help him get the
flowers and so on and so forth, you know.

"Well, he went in the house, and when I seen that
the woman did let him in—I wasn't sure she would or
not—when I seen that she did let him in, I got out,
and I kind of just walked slowly over towards the door
and heard one shot and then there was a pause, and
then I heard two more shots, and I went up and I
walked in the . . . into the front door.

"All I ever got was just right inside the front door,
and I couldn't see very well 'cause I had sunglasses on,
and by the time I got 'em off, I didn't even know which
way he went—I couldn't tell when he went in, you
know, just from where I was sitting in the car, I just
seen him walk in—and I started to go forward and

down some steps, and then I heard a little commotion behind me, and I come out and started that way.

"I could see down the aisle where Larry had dropped the flowers, or the woman had dropped the flowers in the kind of hallway going to the room—I guess was the bedroom right there—I couldn't see very well, my eyes were still focusing, you know. I just caught a glimpse of everything, and I seen Larry going out the front door.

"Well, I thought something was wrong, you know, I thought maybe she might have reached a shotgun or something. I didn't know what had happened, you know, he was just, he was really in kind of like a frenzy, you know, and I found out later he was just nervous and a little, I guess his adrenaline was running, you know, and he got out the front door, he didn't even see me, and I went out right behind him and I said, 'Larry, Larry,' I said, 'What happened?' And he said: 'Let's go, let's go.'

"He was real anxious, and he jumped in the car and like I said I thought something was probably wrong so I didn't go back after the flowers—I was worried about somebody coming around the corner with a shotgun, maybe someone else was in the house or something, I didn't know.

"I didn't really think about him just being scared, and I jumped in the car and we took off, and when we got about a half a block away I said: 'What happened?' And he said, 'Nothing, everything is all right.' And I said: 'Man, you left them flowers in there.' And he said, 'Oh,' he just forgot about them, he said. 'Well, Yankee,' he says, 'She dropped 'em when we first went in the hallway, you know.'

"He said, 'When we first started down the hallway,' he says, 'When I first fired at her' he said, 'I missed her on the first shot, and she dropped the flowers, and she run back into the bedroom' and he said, 'And I chased her back in the bedroom' and he says, 'Where I shot her,' you know, and he said, 'Then I forgot about the flowers.'

"Then I slowed down to get them because, I says, 'I know my fingerprints are on 'em,' and I said, 'They could just trace them right back to me,' you know, and he was still nervous and he said, 'Well, you'll have to go in and get 'em,' he said, 'I'll just have to wait in the car,' and he said, 'And don't be in there too long.'

"So we turned around, and we started back by the house, and there was a woman across the street, and I could tell she was getting a little suspicious because we left the front door kind of ajar, you know—we left in such a hurry, and I was sure she was going towards the house, but evidently she didn't go over there, but we just decided that it was too risky to stop, and we just drove on by, and what I had in back of my mind was, I could probably reach Bill through Lee before he went home, you know, and he could dispose of these flowers."

Hall said he returned to the truck and drove it to the middle of the Interstate 430 bridge and dropped the gun, the sign and the clipboard into the Arkansas River. Then he drove to a coffee shop on Main Street in North Little Rock and tried to call Orsini, but she wasn't home the first time he tried. When she finally answered the phone, she asked him how everything went:

"I said everything went all right, but I said: 'We've got a bad problem.'

"I said: 'My friend left these flowers in the house,' And she said, 'Well,' she said, 'Is everything else all right?'

"She said, 'Where's the gun?' and I said, 'In the river.'

"She said, 'Is everything else gone?' and I said, 'Yes.'

"She says, 'Well, don't worry about the flowers,' she says. 'I can take care of the flowers,' she says, 'Cause

Bill's going to call me,' she says, 'Before he calls the police.' And, she says, 'I'll tell him to dispose of the flowers.'

"And I said: 'Well, make sure he does now because my fingerprints are on 'em.'"

Hall said that one or two nights before, Orsini told him McArthur would raise the price from $20,000 to $25,000, "if we made sure we done it that week because she was having the family come back the following Monday, and she said he even made a joke 'I don't want to spend the Fourth of July weekend with her,' you know—but anyway, he wanted it done Friday, and raised the price up to $25,000. And, like I say, she made that crack about he didn't want to spend the weekend with that son-of-a-bitch or something like that, you know—and, anyway, she told me that she would take care of the flowers."

Hall said McClendon called him on Saturday to tell him the sheriff had been out to his mother's house looking for him. The sheriff had told McClendon's mother he was looking for her son to question him about some stolen cars. When McClendon told Hall he thought the sheriff really wanted to talk to him about the murder, Hall told him, "Nah, there's no heat over this." Hall then remembered the flowers, but he thought Orsini had taken care of that problem.

Hall said that on Sunday, two days after the murder, he went to a private club called the Mason Jar and discovered that Orsini had left a message for him there that everything was all right, and she would soon be in touch with him about what he needed. He understood this to mean she would call him about the money. The message also warned him that he should be careful if he called her at home, "because she figured the phones were hot at her house."

While he was at the Mason Jar, someone came into the bar and said the sheriff was in the parking lot with several other policemen.

". . . it still didn't click on me," Hall told police. "I just thought you all . . . looking for . . . maybe a burglar or something."

He told police that Orsini wanted to make it look like Troutt was responsible for "all this." After he and McClendon took care of Alice, Orsini wanted him to fire shots into the home of James Nelson, McArthur's partner in BJ's.

"And then she wanted me to even go by her house and shoot a couple of bullets through her front door, see. And I said, 'No, I'm not going to be driving all around town with this gun in the car that has just killed someone,' you know. That's why she made up the story I guess about this gold Cadillac driving by her . . . house. . . ."

He told the police and prosecutor that while he and McClendon were in the Little Rock jail, they communicated between the walls of their cells. Hall said McClendon asked him if he had read the paper and seen the news about the flowers being discovered at Alice's feet:

"And he said, 'You know what, Yankee,' he says, 'There was somebody else in that house,' like that. And I went, 'Do what?' and he says, 'Oh, there had to be.' He says, 'Them flowers were moved,' like that. And I said, 'What do you mean the flowers were moved?' And he said, 'Well,' he said, 'She dropped them flowers,' he said, 'In fact, she dropped 'em in the hall, in the hall before she even went in the bedroom or just as she went into the bedroom. . . .'"

"And I says: 'She did?' And he said, 'Yeah,' he says, 'You heard the first shot,' you know, 'cause I mentioned to him I heard one and then the pause—and I said, 'Yeah,' and he said: 'She dropped 'em then and run back into the bedroom.' And he said, 'I chased her back there' and he said, 'Them flowers weren't at her feet.'"

". . . Of course, it clicked on me right away. I said:

'Damn, it had to be Bill, who else could have moved 'em,' you know."

Although Hall had made an earlier statement that when he entered the McArthur home he could "see down the aisle where Larry had dropped the flowers," he now claimed he never actually saw the flowers.

Piazza: "But you didn't see any there right there by the...."

Hall: "No, I couldn't see from there. I never did see the flowers.... I don't know how close to the bedroom. He just said... 'She dropped the flowers,' he said, 'Out in the hall' or 'Out by the hall,' or something like that. Anyway, they were far away from her body, you know."

Robinson interrupted the confession and told Hall he had heard Hall once handled some cocaine for Bill McArthur, but Hall said that was not true. When Robinson asked if McClendon had said exactly where Alice was when she was shot, Hall said he didn't know. "He just said that she was shot in the bedroom, you know, he didn't mention... that she was in the closet, which seems strange, you know. But he didn't say she was shot in the closet."

Piazza asked Hall why he agreed to participate in a violent crime when his past record was nonviolent.

Hall: "I don't know, she just... I don't know, seemed like she had a spell over me or something. I can't figure it out myself, 'cause I've never done anything like this before."

On the day Hall's confession appeared in the newspaper, rumors began circulating around the courthouse that McArthur had killed himself. Both newspapers received calls from people who said they heard he had hanged himself or shot himself. When McArthur got back to his office from lunch that day, a policeman was waiting for him to make sure he was all right. That evening the lawyer appeared on the early news broadcasts of the local television stations to put an end to the rumor.

That same day Robinson reported someone fired at him while he was on his way home from work. Sheriff's department investigators found a crease in his gasoline tank.

Although Robinson was determined his agency would solve the case, the next day Robinson received a court order to turn over the complete case file to the prosecutor and release Yankee Hall to the Little Rock police for questioning. The McArthur murder was their case, but the defendants were being held in the county jail, which is under the supervision of the sheriff's department. Little Rock police Chief Simpson and Assistant Chief Hale were leaving Bentley's office when Robinson stormed in. Television and newspaper reporters had been tipped off about the confrontation and were on hand to record Robinson's arrival. The first person Robinson ran into was Doc Hale:

"You let one thing happen to Hall and it's your butt," Robinson shouted.

Then he spotted Simpson: "Y'all are covering it up," he said.

"You're a disgrace to law enforcement," Simpson replied.

Simpson walked away with Robinson mimicking him in a schoolboy fashion, "You're a disgrace to law enforcement."

His [Hall's] first story was that Lee Orsini had set it up for Bill McArthur . . . I'll say this for him, from the first time he talked to me, all the way through this thing, he never changed his story.

. . . Jess F. "Doc" Hale, 1984

Chapter Eighteen

WHILE A PRISONER IN THE PULASKI County Jail, Lee Orsini frequently used a jail telephone to call Maj. Larry Dill at his private office number. On August 31 and September 1, 1982, several of those telephone calls were tape-recorded by Dill. Transcripts of those calls indicate that Dill, apparently, was attempting to find out whether she would incriminate McArthur.

"...if Lee Orsini told me that Bill McArthur is involved, I'm going to check it out," Dill said during one call.

"I know," Orsini said.

"So?" Dill asked.

Orsini avoided answering the question. So Dill told her about a conversation he had with her attorney, Jack Lessenberry.

"When your attorney sits up here and says, 'Well, I haven't heard anything from my client about Bill McArthur being involved in it.'"

"I don't know why he said that," Orsini said.

"I get to wondering, well, hell, you know. I just don't know, Lee, you know," Dill said.

On the morning of Wednesday, September 1, Orsini again called Dill on his private line:

"I've got something worked out in my mind I want to discuss with you," Orsini said.

"Okay."

"...I want to see what you think of this, I've got a

call in to Jack, and I want to see . . . this will give me some time before, you know, I was sentenced or anything to get Tiffany taken care of, see if y'all are willing to go for this. I'll let Jack talk to the prosecutor and give him the letter that you were talking about last night, you kind of give me a rough draft of what will help you to say, you know, that . . . I will do thus and so at Bill's trial. I let him drop the charges to the same that Bill's is, conspiracy, I mean if this is agreeable to Jack, Jack may want to do something else. Let me plead innocent to it in court for two reasons. Number one, the publicity. I don't want anybody to know except that prosecutor and all that I'm making a deal because, you know, everything . . . I don't know how everything gets in the paper, it's just like . . ."

"Yeah," Dill said.

". . . and that I'm willing to stand trial and if nothing else, Larry, if right before my trial that we just, you know, enter another plea or something but anyway . . . Jack's going to have to work out what I'm really trying to say, maybe you know what I'm trying to say."

"I don't know," Dill said. "If the man just knew that you had knowledge that McArthur was behind it. . . ."

"That's what I'm saying, but I don't want to give a statement as to what I've got knowledge of or anything until, until, you know, until the testimony, but if Jack will . . . if Jack can work it out and back me up with a letter saying, you know, so you can file direct, and you can do your job."

"Well," Dill said, "I think that probably the prosecutor, Lee, in all honesty is going to want to know whether you would testify to the facts in this case. Now that's what he's going to want."

"Oh well, yeah. I mean, . . . Jack's going to have to work it out in legal terms to protect me," Orsini said.

"Yeah, and he's also probably going to want to know if you have personal knowledge of Bill McArthur

being involved or not involved in this case. That's what
he's going to want to know," Dill said.

"Yeah . . . what I'm saying is Jack's gonna have to
work that out, you know, as what can protect me as
well as what y'all want done. . . . I'm not going to ask
for anything that's way out in left field," Orsini said. "I
want Jack to line it out and maybe if he . . . Jack knows
Raff [Gene Raff, one of the candidates being considered as special prosecutor in McArthur's case], and he
likes him. I mean Jack has respect for him, I don't say
he likes him, but he has respect for his ability, and if
he'll do the same thing before the judge that Bill did,
put me on a bond and let me get out on bond until I
can get some things . . . because I could expedite things
so much faster than my mother can as far as getting
stuff sold and getting, you know, getting them another
place to live and everything."

Orsini said she didn't think anybody would be upset
over an arrangement to let her out on bond, "particularly now that Bill's out on bond."

". . . I can understand you wanting to protect yourself, Lee," Dill said, "but at the same time, I think that
the new prosecutor coming on this case . . . he's got to
know whether you can implicate or will implicate Bill
McArthur in this thing."

Dill and Orsini were assuming the special prosecutor
would have the authority to offer her a plea bargain.
However, that authority rested with Pulaski County
Prosecuting Attorney "Dub" Bentley; and, according
to what her attorney, Jack Lessenberry, said later, plea
bargaining was never an issue in Orsini's case. He said
he never discussed plea bargaining with the prosecutor.

In another conversation with Dill, Orsini asked how
Robinson could get control of her case, and Dill told
her if she could submit evidence on McArthur, he
thought a negotiated plea could be worked out for her

through her attorney. She also told Dill she had discussed it with Lessenberry, who had asked her, "Lee, how did he [McArthur] get you to do this?"

"And I said, 'Well, he had an awful lot of leverage' and he said, 'Did it concern your husband's case?' And I said, 'Well, not necessarily the case, but it concerned a piece of evidence.'"

"Well, . . . I told you that if something came up that affected Tiffany, . . . you and I would try to resolve that thing, so," Dill said.

Apparently Orsini either was aware Dill was recording the conversation, or she feared someone might pick up a telephone and listen in, because she never said what it was that might affect Tiffany. In another conversation, however, Orsini made another cloaked reference to Dill about her daughter:

Dill said, ". . . I want to tell you something, you know, you brought up something while ago about telling Jack about that deal with Tiffany, I'm not sure that I wouldn't, I'm not sure that you. . . ."

"I'm going to time it right before I do," Orsini said.

"Oh, yeah, . . . you don't never know when you may need him to help you work out something for her, you know what I mean?"

Still referring to Tiffany, Orsini told Dill that McArthur "really pulled her through" her grieving process after Ron's death.

"Bill did a lot for her too," Orsini said. ". . . Bill had her in that office, and he talked to her and he talked to her, and he talked to her . . . they would never let me know what they talked about. I was told I wasn't allowed to know, and that's when I think he come up with all this information, now he . . . at least he had me convinced that there was a very strong possibility that she could have done it." (There is no evidence to support any connection between Tiffany and Ron Orsini's death, and Lee Orsini may well have been making this statement merely as a smokescreen of some kind.)

* * *

Yankee Hall pleaded guilty on Thursday, September 16, 1982, to a reduced charge of first-degree murder in the slaying of Alice McArthur. He was sentenced to life in prison without parole in exchange for his testimony against Larry McClendon and Lee Orsini.

The next day, in a motion filed in Circuit Court, Dub Bentley announced he would not seek the death penalty against Orsini because she had never before been convicted of a felony.

A few weeks before Orsini's trial, a story appeared in the *Arkansas Democrat* under the byline of "Tery Wolf, Special to the *Democrat*." At that time, Wolf was a television reporter, but two years later she went to work for Robinson.

Her report included pretrial comments made by Special Judge Randall Williams, 58, who was appointed to preside over the trials of all three defendants. Her source was Major Dill of the sheriff's office. Dill allegedly overheard Judge Williams say there was no way McArthur could be convicted of the murder conspiracy charges filed against him. Dill said the remark should have disqualified Williams from hearing the case against the three people charged in Alice McArthur's death.

Dill also alleged—and Wolf reported—that Bentley planned to turn over evidence to defense attorneys and was trying to keep certain witnesses from talking. Wolf said Williams, Bentley and McArthur's attorney, Jack Holt, could not be reached for comment regarding Dill's allegations.

I consider it a damn shame that the true story couldn't come out.

. . . Larry Dill, 1985

Chapter Nineteen

LEE ORSINI PLEADED INNOCENT TO THE charge of capital murder in the death of Alice McArthur, and testimony in her trial began Monday, October 4, 1982 in Little Rock. Hall had already had his day in court, and McClendon's trial would not begin until December. McArthur's hearing to determine whether the sheriff's office had probable cause to arrest him was not scheduled until November.

Spectators crammed into the small courtroom to get a look at the woman who had become one of the state's most well-known figures. She was dressed in a lavender print suit and had her hair gathered into a bun on top of her head. Reporters and courtroom artists packed into a row of seats across from the jurors. A newspaper reporter noted that most of the spectators were middle-aged women.

Hall was brought into the courtroom wearing handcuffs, which were unlocked once he was inside. Before opening arguments he was taken to an area outside the courtroom near where the other witnesses were sequestered.

During opening arguments Chris Piazza, Dub Bentley's chief assistant, who served as the lead trial attorney, used a chalkboard to illustrate a wheel. In the middle of the wheel he wrote "Lee Orsini." He told the jurors Orsini was the hub of a complex plot to arrange Alice McArthur's slaying. At the end of each spoke he wrote the names of Orsini's acquaintances who were to testify. Piazza told the jurors Orsini had spun a story, or web, "that's very difficult to understand and very intricate." He explained she had kept each of her friends isolated from the others so they could not compare the various stories she told.

The prosecution presented its case first, and the state's first witness was Hall, who took the stand for nearly three hours. His testimony consisted primarily of the statements he made in his August 29 confession. He said Lee Orsini had arranged the bombing of Alice's car and the shooting on July 2. He said she helped him plant the bomb on the evening of May 20, and he described the events of the day of the slaying, naming Larry McClendon as the one who pulled the trigger.

In addition to Hall's testimony about recruiting McClendon as the trigger man, the state presented two witnesses who placed McClendon and his gold Cadillac at the crime scene about 4:30 p.m. Four other prosecution witnesses placed McClendon in the company of Yankee Hall the morning of the murder.

Other testimony on the first day of the trial included a statement by Carl Wilson, the construction worker, who said he made the plastic explosive for Hall, and he identified Orsini as the woman who accompanied Hall on the day Hall picked up the explosive. Hall said he introduced Orsini to Wilson as "Suzie" because that was the name she liked to use when she didn't want anybody to know who she was. Wilson described her as having a "pretty butt" and "pretty blue eyes." Wilson said Hall told him he needed the explosive to "blow up some stumps," and Wilson's girlfriend took the stand later and also identified Orsini as the woman who came to Wilson's with Hall.

When Anita Prather was called to testify about finding Alice's body, her testimony cleared up a question which had been raised in the case regarding McArthur's phone call to her:

"He called and wanted to know if I had seen Alice, or had talked to her because, he said, he had come home and couldn't locate her and was worried about her. And, in fact, he said he had called the police and wanted to know if I knew her whereabouts."

"Did you become worried about her?" Piazza asked.

"Yes, I did, very much."

"Was there anything in that conversation that made you worry?"

"Well, his—I could tell he was worried and upset. And he had stated that he had already called the police, and that he had found the dog outside and her purse and shoes were there. And he couldn't locate her, and he said that he was worried, so, that made me worry."

"And did you go to the residence?"

"Well, I, uh, was getting ready to go play tennis. I was just finishing putting on my tennis shoes. And my husband was downstairs, and I went down and I said —I told him about the telephone call. And, uh, I said, 'I think I'll just run down there.' I was getting ready to run down and get some hamburgers for my kids and, so, I thought, 'I'll just run by there on my way,' because I was just worried about her, and it was hard to go about my business without finding out what was happening."

"When you got there, what did you observe?" Piazza asked.

"When I got there, Bill was at the front door, and he let me in. And I was talking to him and he had told me that he had seen a funny thing on the wall, and said that it was a mark or a tear, he said it could even be a bullet hole . . ."

"Did you see a hole in the wall?"

"Yes, I did."

". . . Okay," Piazza said. "Did you go back into the room where Alice was found?"

"Yes."

"Tell me about that if you would."

"Okay. We had been standing right by the bedroom door because that is where the place on the wall was. Some other policemen were coming in the front door, and they—the two men—started back down the hall toward the front door. I stepped inside the bedroom door and was looking at the bed because that is where Alice had folded some clothes. She was packing to go to the lake, I guess. That is what I was told. And I was standing there and looking at the clothes on the bed and thinking about what she had been doing and where she might be, or, you know, what had happened. And I heard the voices and as I turned to go out of the bedroom I turned and passed the open closet door and I saw—all I saw was her legs—from just sort of the bends of both legs. And I didn't—as soon as it registered with me what I saw, I just ran from the room as fast as I could down the hall to where the men were standing."

Joyce Gudmundson, the woman who lived across the street from the McArthurs, said about 4:23 p.m. on July 2 she saw a car enter the McArthurs' steep driveway from the right-hand side.

She testified that she saw a black man get out of the car with a bouquet of flowers. He went to the front door, and she saw Alice open the glass storm door and saw the McArthurs' poodle run outside. She turned away, but when she looked back a few seconds later, no one was at the door. Then she saw the driver get out of the car and walk to the door. She described him as a white man with "grayish" hair. Gudmundson turned away again, but she looked back at the McArthur home a few minutes later and saw both men in the car. The car attempted to back out of the steep driveway but didn't quite make it on the first try. On the second try, the car came out of the driveway, and as it turned to go down the street, Gudmundson looked for a license number because she had become more alert to activities at the house since the bombing of Alice's car. She remembered thinking it was odd that the car had no license plate.

Various police officers, including Dawson, the first Little Rock detective on the scene, testified regarding evidence taken from the crime scene. On cross-examination Lessenberry asked Dawson about isolation of the crime scene, and Dawson explained that several law enforcement officers were at the McArthur home by the time he arrived. He said Officer McNeely had secured the house on the inside and all the Pulaski County officers were outside.

Dr. Fahmy Malak, the state medical examiner, said he performed an autopsy on July 4 which showed Alice died instantaneously from a single bullet fired almost at point-blank range through the crown of her head:

"When she was brought to you, did she still have a pen in her hand?" Piazza asked.

"Yes," Malak said. "When I examined Mrs. McArthur, she was holding a black pen in her left hand which I took from her hand, and I released it to the trace evidence section of the Crime Lab."

"Dr. Malak, is it unusual for a person to grasp that type of item and hold it after death?"

"Well . . . no, it is not unusual. We see this in many occasions. Prior to death, if somebody is excited or in some sort of activity, the person may die and remain holding what is in the hand. This is a known phenomenon in legal medicine, it is called cadaveric spasm, the clasping firmly upon the object, the hand stays as such. So, it is a usual finding."

"Would you please demonstrate . . . where the bullet entered Mrs. McArthur's head and the path that it took?"

"The bullet went through the back of the head, on the left side above the left ear, and traveled down and to the right, and lodged around the middle ear on the right side. The bullet was traveling about forty-five degrees from back to front, left to right, and downwards."

Phoebe Pinkston testified about a conversation with Lee Orsini in the last week of June, during which she had let it slip that the McArthur children were out of town at camp. She also testified Orsini had insinuated she had some type of relationship with Bill McArthur, but Phoebe said she thought McArthur treated Orsini just as a good friend and client.

She also testified that after she left work on July 2, she went to her husband's pawn shop. She said Orsini called her there about 5:15 p.m. and during their conversation Orsini asked her to hold on while she answered the door. When Orsini returned to the telephone, she told Phoebe there was a black man at her door carrying a box, but she would not open the door. According to her testimony, the call from Orsini came about an hour before the news of Alice's murder was broadcast.

Other testimony that day consisted of a microcassette tape the police had removed from the McArthur telephone. After the bombing of Alice's car in May, the McArthurs taped any incoming calls, except those from family and friends. The next to the last call on the tape was the voice of a woman who said, "Mom, Mom. Sorry. I have the wrong number." Alice said, "All right" and hung up. Pinkston and Diane Dutton, the receptionist, identified the caller's voice as Orsini's.

James Handloser, security manager for Southwestern Bell Telephone Company and former FBI agent, had a list of all the calls trapped on the McArthur phone on July 2. He testified four calls were traced that Friday from Orsini's home to the McArthur residence. Those incoming calls from Orsini's unlisted number were recorded at 12:17, 12:21, 1:40, and 1:59 p.m.

A trap, unlike a wiretap or other listening device,

traps an incoming call and records the point of origination. It does not record conversation. A trap works only if the exchange for that originating telephone number has previously been "activated." An exchange is not activated until the phone company installs a special program in the computer at the central office for that exchange to report where the calls are originating. All a trap does at this point is tell the phone company which exchange originated the call. Once the computer program is installed in the central exchange, all subsequent calls from that exchange can be traced to the originating telephone numbers. The day after the bombing McArthur had requested the trap be put on his home telephone, and the initial trap on the McArthur phone only recorded the entire phone numbers from the exchange that served the McArthurs' part of town. It also could record calls from other exchanges but not entire phone numbers, only prefixes. As time went on, however, various other exchanges were "activated" so entire numbers from those exchanges could be trapped.

Handloser explained that traps cannot determine whether a call was answered, but that they could determine whether the line was busy.

Hall already had testified he called the McArthur home in the early afternoon of July 2 from a service station and Alice answered and he asked for "John Allen." Handloser's records showed a call at 2:16 p.m. from a 372 exchange, but the entire number was not identified due to computer trouble in the telephone system.

"And is the Gulf station here on Broadway in that exchange?"

"Yes, sir, it is."

Hall said he then called Orsini, and she told him she knew Mrs. McArthur was home because she had just called her.

Handloser also testified a call from the Wulz residence was made to Orsini's telephone at 6:47 a.m. on May 21, the day Alice's car was bombed.

"Now, a trap was on her line also?"

"Yes, Mrs. Orsini came to my office on March 2 and requested a trap and signed the form."

"Did she subsequently get another number?"

"Yes, sir. On March 16, there was a second line installed at that address listed for T.R. Orsini."

"Did she request a trap on her second line?"

"No, sir, she did not."

"So, you would not have calls coming to her on the second line?"

"No, sir."

Testimony was introduced regarding the purchase of the floral arrangement. An employee of Leroy's Flowers identified a photograph showing a floral centerpiece she had made for a male customer shortly after 4 p.m. on July 2.

Joyce Holt, one of Lee's friends, unrelated to attorney Jack Holt, also testified Tuesday as a state's witness. She said Orsini had told her in February that she and Bill McArthur were having an affair.

Mrs. Holt said Orsini had asked her to rent a room for her at a motel in North Little Rock so she and McArthur could use it to meet with someone from the sheriff's office. She said Orsini had also asked her to testify that she had seen McArthur's car in the motel parking lot the evening the reservation was made, although she had not actually seen it.

Mrs. Holt said Orsini told her she had received an anonymous telephone call a week before the bombing of Alice's car from someone who told her there would be a bombing. And she said Orsini also told her Alice was having an affair with Bob Troutt, and that Sheriff Tommy Robinson had taped a statement by Mrs. McArthur admitting the affair.

Then the prosecution's prime evidence was introduced. Larry Burge, the man who helped Orsini make the phony tape-recording about Alice's murder, took the stand:

"Did you have occasion to call the Pulaski County Sheriff's office on July 4, 1982, Mr. Burge?"

"Yes, I did."

"Why did you call them?"

"Lee had called me at my home and told me that she needed for me to come down and talk with her. I had some people over visiting or something, but anyway I went on down because I felt like that it was urgent that I do go talk with her, and after going down to my office where Lee was, she gave me some information and told me that this information had been given to her by a telephone tipper, and that it was information that she felt like would be good for the police department—the sheriff's department—to have in trying to apprehend whomever had done this crime."

"And what was this information that she gave you?"

"On that day she gave me a telephone number and an address and a name."

"What was that name?"

"Larry McClendon."

"And what did she ask you to do?"

"She asked me to call into the sheriff's department and tell them that—anonymously—that Mr. McClendon was the person who had killed Mrs. McArthur."

"Did you do that?"

"Yes, I did."

"And how many times did you call?"

"I talked to the sheriff's department three times that day. . . ."

"Did you have occasion to see Mrs. Orsini on Monday, July 5?"

"Yes, I did . . . I had either called Lee or she had called me that morning and told me at that time that she had had more information come in—that someone had called her and given her more information pertaining to the murder, and she wanted me to come by her house and talk with her, and so I did."

"And when you went by there did she give you anything?" Piazza asked.

"Yes, she showed me some notes that she had taken down from the telephone call that she said that she had received and had the information jotted down on these—on the yellow pages of a paper. . . ."

"Did you have any discussion at that time as to why she couldn't tell the sheriff's department?"

"I believe that on that date she wanted me to make a tape and give this information where it would be recorded and that she could turn it in to the sheriff's department. There was a discussion as to credibility or that it would be better if it came in as an anonymous tip—it might be acted on faster or something."

"In other words, she left you with the understanding that it would be better for you to do it anonymously than for her to go to them and tell them what she had heard."

"Yes. And this would also keep me out of the paper and things like that."

"Did she mention anything about a credibility problem?"

"I believe that on that day that she told me that she wasn't sure that the police department would believe her—that there was a credibility problem."

Burge testified he went to a pay phone on Monday, July 5 and called Orsini and read the information off the script she had provided, but when he went by her house later in the day, he discovered the tape had broken so he had to do it all over again.

"I took the notes and got back in my car and went and found another phone and called again. . . ."

"And did you use those same notes she had given you that morning?"

"Yes, I did."

"What was it?"

"Well, the information that she said that the sheriff's department needed was to reiterate the accusation against Mr. McClendon and to name Mrs. Alice McArthur and Mrs. Holly Troutt and Mrs. Lee Orsini as three persons who were supposedly on a hit list in the Little Rock area and what the—and give an explanation as to why these women were on the list."

"Did she mention anybody else besides Larry McClendon being the killer?"

"She had mentioned to me that Mr. McClendon had a white, male running buddy. . . ."

"Did she indicate any fear?"

"Well, she told me that someone had come to her house on the day of the killing—the day that Mrs. McArthur was killed—and had driven up to her driveway and came to her door with a box."

"Did she indicate being fearful on Monday, July 5?"

"Yes."

"Was this a reason for furnishing the identity of these two people to law enforcement?"

"Yes. My impression was that, you know, that this person needed to be taken off the street because of her own safety."

"And you felt like you were performing a service by assisting in getting this information to law enforcement authorities, didn't you, Mr. Burge?"

"Yes. I knew they could run this down and find out if it is valid real quick."

Burge said on the morning of July 16, the day Orsini was arrested, he took her to the office of Rita Gruber, an attorney who was handling a few civil matters for Orsini. From there he went to the Little Rock Police Department, and Orsini knew he was going to the police station.

When he left the LRPD about 12:30 p.m., he called Orsini at Rita Gruber's office and told her they needed to have "a very serious talk." She agreed to meet Burge at Dr. Wulz's apartment at 1:30 p.m., but she wasn't there when he arrived. When he finally tracked her down at a Shoney's Restaurant in North Little Rock, he asked her to go with him to talk to the police, but she refused.

Burge also testified Orsini told him Alice McArthur and Bob Troutt were having an affair. He said Orsini said Bill McArthur told her about the affair, and he testified he saw Wulz carrying a gun the day of the bombing of Alice's car.

Before Burge left the witness stand, Bentley played the tape that Burge and Orsini had recorded:

Burge: "You also have to realize that I don't want my picture in the paper along with yours tomorrow."

Orsini: "That's not funny."

Burge: "It wasn't intended to be a pun, okay. A gentleman by the name of Mr. Forrest Parkman. . . ."

Orsini: "Okay."

Burge: "—is well into crime in the area, it seems, and he is the gentleman that asked these other two gentlemen to call on you and Mrs. Holly Troutt and Mrs.—I keep forgetting the lady's name—Mrs. McArthur. And Mr. Forrest Parkman . . . also, he is interested in race horses. I think he owns a couple or three or maybe a dozen—I don't know. But he does own some race horses . . . I've read earlier in the paper where you were working with the North Little Rock Police Department which seems to have backfired on you completely, and everything, this Mr. Parkman also is a friend of Mr. Bill Younts."

Orsini: "[North Little Rock Police] Chief Younts."

Burge: "Yes, this is correct."

Orsini: "What does Parkman do?"

Burge: "I do not know what he does. I know he is into horse races. He may be independently wealthy, who knows. But he is very interested in night clubs and gambling and things like this. In fact, the information I have—the big problems actually started over the nightclub business."

Orsini: "I'm not involved in the nightclub business."

Burge: "Well, you were involved in something, or your husband was involved in something a year or so ago because he, too, was killed. Is this correct?"

Orsini: "That's right. What do you know about that?"

Burge: "I don't know anything about it other than what I've read in the papers, and no one seems to know very much about it. . . ."

Orsini: "Then why would they want to kill me?"

Burge: "Because it seems that you keep things stirred up. You just continually muddy the water, and as the man said, you won't let things die, and Mrs. Troutt knows entirely too much."

Orsini: "Why was Mrs. McArthur killed?"

Burge: "Mrs. McArthur was killed because she knew too much, also."

Orsini: "What do you mean, Mrs. McArthur knew too much, also."

Burge: "I don't know. You know, she's the [wife] of the lawyer. Perhaps he had been discussing his matters at home. I do not know the man. I don't know if that was his habit or not, but if it was, it was unfortunate."

Orsini: "That doesn't make sense."

Burge: "Okay. There was going to—let me just—I have some notes here, actually . . . I had talked to the police on numerous occasions yesterday trying to get something going. . . ."

Orsini: "You talked to the police department or the sheriff's department?"

Burge: "Sheriff's department. I wouldn't call the police department after I found out about a man by the name of Mike Willingham on the police department . . . it seems that Mr. Willingham and Mr. Parkman are friends. And it seems like that Mr. Willingham may be working on your case at this time, and if he is. . . ."

Orsini: "On my case?"

Burge: "Yes, . . . you can't mention Troutt without thinking of Orsini."

Orsini: "Do you know anything about any connections?"

Burge: "I'm just—I'm giving you what I have. Don't confuse me because these notes are very poorly written, and I had hoped that I wouldn't have to do this. It's been a long day already even though it is still early. Okay. But you might check with someone on Mr. Mike Willingham and check his connection with Mr. Parkman . . . , and you might check out the name that I gave you earlier on Mr. McClendon, and you might do anything you can in the world to try to keep these things out of the newspaper because they are very, very obviously trying to set you up for something."

The script also called for the possibility someone would bring in a "new talent" or "large talent to take care of the sheriff."

Orsini: "Why are you calling us and telling us this?"

Burge: "Because you need to get someone to help you out, lady. If you do not do this you are going to be dead as a thousand-year-old mummy."

Orsini: "Well, the sheriff is helping. I'm very confident in Tommy Robinson and Larry Dill."

To back up Burge's contention that the script was written by Orsini, the prosecutor brought in a handwriting analyst from the State Crime Laboratory who said the script matched samples of Orsini's handwriting.

Bill McArthur was the last prosecution witness on Tuesday. He told how he first became involved in representing Orsini, then he was asked about the events of the summer of 1981 when he became involved in plans to open a nightclub:

"Did you have the opportunity or did you discuss the possibility of the defendant becoming involved in that organization?" Piazza asked.

"Well, the discussion was of what we were doing—

just a mention that we were—James Nelson, Bob Robbins, and I—what we were planning on doing, and it did evolve into some discussion of her becoming involved . . . the first thing she mentioned to me was that she had some friends that might be interested in investing some money or loaning some money for such a venture. All of their names I don't recall—later on, that more or less passed out of existence, and she then talked about the possibility of her borrowing some money on some land that she owned or some property that she had and investing or loan the money to the corporation."

"And did that come about?"

"No, it did not."

When asked if Alice took an active role in the organization of the club, he said she had.

"Yes, all of our wives did, as a matter of fact."

"Did you present the proposition to the members of this organization, including your wife, of the possibility Lee Orsini would become involved?"

"Yes, I did."

"What was the reaction?"

"Well, it's difficult to say there was a reaction."

"Let me phrase it this way. After you proposed or at least made the proposal to your partners, was Ms. Lee Orsini accepted in the organization?"

"No."

"Now, did she also discuss with you the possibility of doing work for this new organization—this club?"

"Yes. She told me—of course, I knew this because of my representation of her, that she had worked in the advertising field and that she had some friends that she would talk to and see if they had any ideas that would be helpful to us. I don't know the lady that she talked to, but she told me that she had talked to a woman in advertising and brought me a sort of a proposal-type thing with the name of a club and some other matters on it."

"What type of name did she bring to you, do you recall?"

"Yes. The name was 'Tumbleweed.'"

McArthur said none of Orsini's ideas were ever incorporated into his club. In fact, another advertising agency was hired to do the work.

Finally, McArthur testified about his activities on July 2 and his telephone conversation with Alice about 12:20 p.m. He said they talked about their plans for the weekend, and she asked him to come home as early as possible so he could try on some new shorts. The store where she had purchased the shorts closed at 5:30 p.m., and she wanted to return them that afternoon if they didn't fit, he said.

Piazza asked him about his meeting in his office the afternoon of July 2 with Lee Orsini and had McArthur tell what occurred when he arrived home that afternoon. Piazza also asked McArthur about his relationship with Orsini, and McArthur denied ever having an affair with her.

Two days later, the *Arkansas Democrat* printed an analysis of McArthur's testimony headlined, MCARTHUR QUERIED, BUT NOT AS SUSPECT; QUESTIONS UNASKED, which raised more doubt about his innocence.

The analysis reported that the state "avoided asking him any questions that might hint to the jury he also has been charged in his wife's slaying." The article raised several questions about McArthur's guilt or innocence and raised doubt about the motives of the prosecutor by stating that McArthur was not asked if he had helped arrange his wife's murder, had anything to do with the bombing of her car, arranged for his children to be gone on the day of the bombing, changed his clothes when he got home on July 2, or moved the floral arrangement used as a ruse for the gunman to enter the house.

The article also noted: "Maj. Larry Dill of the Pulaski County Sheriff's office—one of the first officers to arrive at the McArthur home on the day of the slaying—was not called to testify. In fact, Little Rock detectives ordered Dill and other county officers out of the house so they could take over the investigation."

I could not even conceive of the amount of fear and horror that those children were living with every day . . . Bill was being threatened at every turn, and he had the responsibility of carrying those children through the whole ordeal, and every day they lived in fear that not only were they going to have to live without their mother, but their father was going to be ripped from them just like she was.

. . . Anita Prather, 1985

Chapter Twenty

THE PROSECUTION RESTED ITS CASE ON Tuesday, October 5, after calling 26 witnesses and introducing 38 pieces of evidence. The defense called fifteen witnesses, but Orsini was not one of them. She never testified on her own behalf. Dr. Charles Wulz was the main witness for the defense, and under direct examination by Lessenberry, Wulz said he and Lee Orsini dated frequently. He said on May 20, the day before the bombing, they went to see an Arkansas Repertory Theatre production and afterward they went to her home where she changed into tennis shoes and jogging clothes, then they went to his house. He said both she and Tiffany spent the night there.

On cross-examination, Chris Piazza asked Wulz why a call had been traced from his house to Orsini's residence at 6:47 a.m. on the day of the bombing if Orsini had stayed at Wulz's house overnight.

Wulz explained that early that morning, May 21, Orsini had jogged back to her home from his, but he said he did not know why she went home.

Wulz also testified that a .38-caliber Smith and Wesson pistol disappeared from his home between June 26 and July 10. The bullet that killed Alice as well as two other slugs found in the McArthur home were .38-caliber Monarch bullets, and the state believed Wulz's gun could have been the murder weapon and had introduced into evidence a box of .38-caliber Federal Monarch shells belonging to Wulz.

Wulz contended he kept the gun loaded with five shells, and he said he gave investigators the box containing the remaining shells, which were manufactured from 1956 to 1975 and had been out of production since then. An unusual characteristic of those type of bullets is a hollowed-out base.

During his testimony about the gun, Wulz said, "...I never fired it, didn't even try it out, bought a box of shells for it, loaded it, and laid it in the dresser drawer. It stayed there, always, in that dresser drawer until, I think, it was just immediately after the grand jury about the Orsini thing that Bill McArthur told—or Lee Orsini—told me that Bill McArthur said that a lady called from a liquor store to say that there was a hit man coming from Louisiana, and I started carrying a gun. It frightened me, mostly for her, but it frightened me a little bit for me...."

Wulz said he and Orsini had sexual relations "on a regular basis." On Monday, Hall had testified that he, too, had sexual relations with Orsini. After Hall said he had been intimate with her, he was asked if she had any distinguishing characteristics, and he said she didn't. In order to rebut Hall's statement about his intimacy with Orsini, Wulz was asked the same thing, and he replied she had a scar on her right hip that could only be seen when she was unclothed.

Wulz said he had been dating Lee Orsini since March 30, 1981, three weeks after Ron Orsini was found shot to death.

The defense called Phoebe Pinkston back to the stand to testify that on the day after the car bombing she had told Orsini about the trap on the McArthur phone, which raised the question of why Orsini would call the McArthur home on the afternoon of the murder if she knew about the trap.

The defense also called a retired telephone company employee who had been taken to Orsini's home by a defense attorney in order to check the automatic dialer

on her phone. The man said one of the phone numbers
that had been programmed into the automatic dialer
was the McArthur home. The implication the defense
was trying to make was that Orsini was trying to call
her mother on July 2 and accidentally dialed the
McArthur residence numerous times. Although it
never came out during Orsini's trial, McArthur
claimed he never told her the police had wiretapped
her home telephone, yet she told Phoebe he had.

Tiffany Orsini testified that she had seen Yankee
Hall at her home one time when he was there to fix the
window on her mother's car after it had been shot out.
She said he asked to use the restroom, and she took
him upstairs to her bathroom. She said the only man
her mother had gone out with during the last year was
Wulz, and Tiffany said she and Tamara Wulz were best
friends. On cross examination, Piazza asked Tiffany
about her relationship with Wulz. He asked if she
trusted him very much:

"No, sir."

"You don't trust him?"

"I don't trust anybody . . . Well, except for my
mother."

During his closing argument Thursday Piazza used a
chalk board beside the jury box to draw an illustration
similar to the one he had drawn during his opening
statement. He drew a web with Orsini's name in the
middle and the names of key figures in the case in
other parts of the web, the names of people Piazza said
she had deceived with lies: Bill McArthur, Larry
Burge, Charles Wulz, Phoebe Pinkston, and Joyce
Holt.

Piazza said Orsini had "spun an intricate web" with
lies. Then, after repeating the phrase she had "drawn a
web" several times, Piazza whipped off his jacket and
used it to erase the web-like drawing on the chalkboard. He turned back to face the jury and said,

"There's another name—Alice McArthur. Don't forget her." The spectators in the courtroom applauded.

After eight hours of deliberation, the jury found Orsini guilty of capital murder. About 9:30 p.m., Judge Randall Williams sentenced Lee Orsini to life in prison without parole.

Tiffany Orsini made the first sound after the verdict was read—she sobbed loudly as she was embraced by her aunt. Orsini, who seemed surprised at the verdict, sank back into her chair and closed her eyes. After the verdict was read and sentence passed, Orsini was taken into the judge's chambers, where she broke into tears. A short time later, still in tears, she was handcuffed and taken back to the county jail by Major Dill.

Lee's gonna get out of there. She's just positive of that. . . . I think the federal courts will let her out because this is an atrocity.

. . . Dr. Charles Wulz, 1984

Chapter Twenty-One

THE NEXT DAY SHERIFF ROBINSON TOLD the media he was "brushing away the cobwebs" to trap the central figures behind the slaying. On the same day, Orsini fired Jack Lessenberry and hired another lawyer, Tom Donovan, to represent her in post-trial proceedings. She said she was "bewildered" by Lessenberry's defense of her.

While people were wondering about McArthur's alleged involvement in his wife's death, it was learned his children were the sole heirs to their mother's estate, including the oil-producing land in Louisiana, and that McArthur could not spend any of the money without approval of the court and Alice's brother, Leonard Miller. Under Louisiana law, if a spouse inherits land, it remains separate property and is not shared with the other spouse. If the owner of the property dies without a will, as Alice did, the children of the owner become the sole heirs.

Within a few days following Orsini's conviction, a Little Rock television station received a letter, purportedly from a state prison inmate, alleging there was a plot to kill Orsini once she was transferred to the prison from the county jail. Because of this threat, she was allowed to remain at the county jail under the protection of the sheriff's department, and on Wednesday, October 20, Robinson said Orsini would not be safe if she were transferred to the state prison.

On Friday Dr. Charles Wulz was called to the prosecuting attorney's office and advised of his rights, but Wulz refused to make a statement and was allowed to leave.

At a hearing the following Monday, Judge Williams ruled Orsini could stay at the county jail because of the death threat. It came out during the hearing that after her trial Orsini had called one of the members of the jury which convicted her. The call was made from the county jail the previous Friday. Judge Williams said he had received other complaints about Orsini calling witnesses, and he instructed Robinson not to let her make calls to anyone except family members and her attorneys. Robinson protested, saying federal court standards allowed inmates unlimited access to telephones. But the judge reminded him that Orsini's situation was different because she had been found guilty, and most county jail inmates were simply awaiting trial.

On Tuesday, October 26, Robinson appeared on a radio talk show and claimed that Chris Piazza, deputy prosecuting attorney who tried the Orsini case, had a friend on the jury which had convicted Orsini. Robinson said Piazza had made a mockery of the criminal justice system. In an apparent attempt to defend Orsini, he said he had checked the records at the sheriff's office and not found any record of a call from Orsini to a juror. He also said Orsini told him her attorneys would not allow her to testify at her trial, even though she wanted to do so.

The next day Piazza held a news conference and said that during jury selection one of the selected jurors admitted he knew both Piazza and Orsini's trial attorney, Jack Lessenberry. The juror said he had served previously as a juror in a case prosecuted by Piazza and had once run into him on a municipal golf course.

Around 6 p.m. that evening Robinson again was interviewed by the radio station. During that interview Robinson discussed his feud with the prosecutor over the handling of the McArthur case and then warned Prosecuting Attorney Dub Bentley to be careful because the sheriff had been keeping him "under surveillance." The next morning Judge Williams, apparently upset by all the publicity regarding the Orsini case, ordered Orsini transfered "forthwith—and by forthwith I mean this afternoon" to the state prison.

Before leaving for prison that Thursday, Orsini told reporters she had given her attorney a written sealed statement about the death of Alice McArthur, "whom I did not have killed." The statement was to be opened in the event of her death.

On Friday, October 29, Judge David Hale, who was to preside over McArthur's probable cause hearing in November, issued a gag order prohibiting public comment by anyone connected with the case. Also on Friday it was learned Robinson had told a group of high school students a week earlier that the state had "no case" against Lee Orsini. He also told them the criminal justice system in Pulaski County "stinks."

Prosecuting Attorney Bentley later took a sworn statement from a woman who was an inmate at the county jail while Orsini was there. The woman, who had hot-check charges against her at the time she made the statement, claimed Orsini had offered her a bribe to give false testimony at McArthur's upcoming probable cause hearing scheduled for November 22:

"She wanted me to testify that my ex-husband sold Bill McArthur cocaine," the woman told Bentley.

"And you told her that you didn't have any knowledge of that, if he did?"

"Yeah. So I told her that me and my husband had been divorced four years...."

"...And did she offer you anything to testify that way?"

"Five thousand dollars...She asked me what I wanted to do when I got over this mess, and I told her I didn't know...so, we got to talking about it, about my two kids and everything, and she said, 'Well, $5,000 would help you a whole lot, wouldn't it?' I said, 'Sure.' And she goes, 'I think I can arrange for $5,000 if you could handle this for me.'"

The woman said Orsini also talked with her about her relationship with Bill McArthur:

"She felt as long as Mrs. McArthur was there, you know, they didn't have any kind of relationship going between her and Bill. She had a lot of words for Mrs. McArthur."

". . . She [Orsini] was in love with him?"

"Yeah."

"And then he didn't respond, do you think that was what that was?"

"That's the impression I got. She said that she couldn't cope with no more rejection."

The woman claimed Orsini also talked about her relationship with Yankee Hall:

"And, she says, '. . . he's not bad looking, he's better in bed.'"

". . . You got the impression that he had been a boyfriend then?"

"Right."

"And that she didn't know how to help him . . . ?"

"She said there wasn't nothing she could do to help him because it would mess her up with her boyfriend Charles . . . That was all she had going for her right now."

She said Orsini told her McArthur was responsible for his wife's death, and Larry McClendon and Yankee Hall would not have been caught if it hadn't been for some flowers. The woman also claimed Orsini had received special treatment while a prisoner at the county jail. Bentley asked the woman if Orsini stayed in Major Dill's office or if she stayed in the "pod," an open area where prisoners could mingle with each other.

"Somewhere else . . . I don't know whose office or if

anybody's office, but she was somewhere all the time. . . ."

The woman said Orsini didn't even eat with the other prisoners.

". . . How long would she be gone when she was taken out?"

"She would leave before dinner, about 4:30, sometimes she would still be gone out when we went to bed at twelve."

On November 1, the *Arkansas Gazette* quoted John J. Erny, Jr. of Larose, Louisiana, the attorney who was handling Alice's estate, as saying Bill McArthur knew since 1975 that his wife's interest in oil-producing land in Louisiana would go to her two children if she died.

Bentley noticed strange things started happening after Orsini was convicted. His house was at the end of a private drive that was rarely traveled by anyone except his family, yet while the Orsini trial was in progress, vehicles started turning around in his drive at night. After two men came to his door one evening—one white and one black—to ask directions, and after he found a shotgun shell in his mailbox one morning, he decided someone was trying to scare him.

One morning one of my dogs had a round hole in his shoulder. I presume it was a gunshot wound . . . a lady moved into a house 150 yards away from mine; she brought her phone with her, and when she plugged it in—before the telephone company hooked it up—she could intercept all of my calls.

> . . . Wilbur C. "Dub" Bentley, 1984
> Pulaski County Prosecuting Attorney

Chapter Twenty-Two

ORSINI AND HALL WERE BROUGHT TO Judge David Hale's municipal courtroom Monday, November 22, 1982, for McArthur's probable cause hearing, a judicial proceeding used to determine whether there is enough evidence against a defendant to hold him for trial. At such a hearing, all the prosecution must do is present enough evidence to convince the judge that there is reasonable cause to send the case to trial. The prosecution does not have to prove the truth of the charges against the defendant, but the defendant is entitled to cross-examine witnesses and attack any evidence presented by the prosecution. McArthur had entered an innocent plea.

Orsini and Hall stayed in a witness room adjacent to the courtroom during the hearing. Other witnesses in the room, including Phoebe Pinkston, noticed Orsini enjoyed being the center of attention. She was joking and laughing with people, and at one point when a local restaurant owner brought in sweet potato pies to serve the witnesses, Orsini played hostess, cheerfully passing out slices of pie. Anita Prather noticed Dill put his arm around Orsini and hugged her when he came into the room. Orsini's behavior was sickening, Prather said later. She could not comprehend why her friend's convicted killer was being treated like a celebrity, and Prather wasn't the only witness disturbed by the display. Phoebe was outraged. When she returned to the witness room after testifying, she stormed toward Orsini:

"You good-for-nothing no-good whore," Phoebe shouted.

Larry Burge stepped between the two women and pulled Phoebe aside before she reached Orsini.

"Well," Orsini said, "what's Phoebe so upset at me about?"

McArthur was represented by a team of four lawyers headed by Jack Holt, who had a reputation as one of the best trial lawyers in the state. Jack Lassiter assisted the defense, as did Bill and Esther Putman of Fayetteville. McArthur's father, Bryan, had known Bill Putman for years, and when McArthur was arrested, he called Putman for help.

Special Prosecutor Sonny Dillahunty's two main witnesses on the first day of the hearing were Bobby L. Blair and George W. Bynum. Blair testified that a few weeks before the slaying he saw a black man at McArthur's law office whom he thought was Larry McClendon. But after cross-examination Blair, who admitted he had been diagnosed as a paranoid schizophrenic, finally said he was confused and not at all positive about what had happened. Bynum testified he had seen McArthur, Orsini, Hall and McClendon together on an elevator in the Union National Bank Building in Little Rock just a few days before Alice was killed. Bynum said he had recognized McArthur because the lawyer had defended two policemen eight years earlier in a civil rights suit filed by Bynum. Bynum had accused the officers of brutality, but he lost the case.

Another witness presented by Dillahunty that day was Ann Harper, who formerly worked as a waitress for Bob Troutt but at the time of her testimony worked at a liquor store owned by Troutt's wife. Harper said she saw McArthur with Lee Orsini in Troutt's club sometime in 1981.

Dillahunty called a Little Rock police officer who testified he responded to a report of a burglary at the McArthur law office on September 1, 1981. Among the missing items was a .38-caliber Smith and Wesson pistol.

Dillahunty, trying to establish a meeting between McArthur and Orsini at a Hot Springs motel, called the manager of the Lake Hamilton Holiday Inn, who said his record showed a "Lee M. Orsini" rented a room for the night of June 9.

Also testifying on Monday was Al Dawson, the Little Rock police detective who was in charge of the Alice McArthur crime scene. Dillahunty raised several questions about the crime scene in an apparent effort to discredit the Little Rock Police Department's investigation. He implied Alice was not killed in the closet, and he also implied Dawson was negligent in not having ballistic tests conducted on the gun found on the shelf of the closet and on a gun recovered from McArthur's car. Dillahunty requested the tests after he was appointed special prosecutor, but the tests indicated that neither gun killed Alice.

Dr. Fahmy Malak again testified about the fatal gunshot wound in the crown of Alice's head, as he had during Orsini's trial, and on cross-examination Malak said Robinson and Dill had come to his house to discuss the pen in Alice's left hand. Holt asked Malak if Robinson and Dill were arguing Alice could not have been shot in the closet, and Malak said they were.

"Did they want to substitute their opinion for yours?" Holt asked.

"This is true," Malak said.

On Tuesday, the second day of the probable cause hearing, Fred Hensley, one of the police detectives working on the case, waited in the witness room for his

turn to testify. Hensley thought nothing was more bor-
ing than sitting in a witness room. He already had read
the newspaper from front to back and was anxious to
get back to work. Noticing the sheriff and Tom Donovan, Orsini's attorney, engrossed in conversation, he
overheard Orsini's name mentioned a few times. He
thought this was odd because he knew everyone in the
witness room was under the rule imposed by the court
not to discuss the case among themselves. Hensley
heard Donovan tell Robinson, "Lee will do whatever
we tell her to do."

Hensley did not report the remark to the judge. Instead, he mentioned it in casual conversation to his
captain at the Little Rock Police Department. The
captain told Chief Simpson, and Simpson reported it
to Dub Bentley, who in turn told Judge Hale. Hale was
upset with Hensley for not reporting it to him immediately. He questioned Hensley's timing and said he
would not permit the feud between the two law enforcement agencies to interfere with the hearing. Donovan denied making the remark.

Orsini took the stand the second day of the probable
cause hearing and testified that she and McArthur had
gone to Memphis, Tennessee together to see a hypnotist, Dr. William M. Foote, after Ron's death.

"What happened after you returned from the trip?"

"Bill climbed into my attic, found a gun, he wrapped
it in a towel and took it with him, and I've never seen
the gun since."

Dillahunty asked Orsini if she had any knowledge of
an agreement between McArthur and Hall to cause
the murder of Alice. She replied she knew there was
such an agreement, but when Dillahunty attempted
further questioning, she took the Fifth Amendment.

Holt attempted to cross-examine her regarding any
knowledge she had concerning McArthur's participa-
tion in a conspiracy to kill his wife. She invoked the

Fifth Amendment more than two dozen times during Holt's questioning, and he moved the court strike her testimony because it deprived the defendant his right of cross-examination, a guarantee of the Sixth Amendment. Judge Hale agreed.

Dr. William M. Foote, the hypnotherapist, testified a man resembling McArthur—but who wore a mustache—accompanied Orsini to his office in Memphis in the spring or summer of 1981. Foote hypnotized her so she could recall where she had seen or placed a pistol. McArthur's position was that he did not accompany Orsini to Memphis, and his attorneys attacked Foote's credentials and brought out the fact he once worked as a stage hypnotist under the name "Merril the Master Hypnotist."

Anita Prather testified about arriving at the McArthurs' house and finding Alice's body. She said reports that McArthur had asked her to come to the house were wrong. She said she decided to stop there on her way to buy some hamburgers. Both Prather and Officer McNeely testified they did not see the floral arrangement near the body.

Leonard Miller, Alice's brother, testified as a defense witness Wednesday, stating his brother-in-law did not stand to profit from Alice's death. He said he and Alice had received less than $5,000 each annually from the oil leases and about $50,000 between them in January, 1982. Both he and Alice received checks for half of the royalties. He also said McArthur did not have a mustache in the summer of 1981.

James Nelson, part owner of BJ's, testified Alice objected to Orsini's investing or being involved in the nightclub. He said McArthur never discussed giving Orsini a job at the club, and he said McArthur was not upset when Orsini's offer to invest in the club was rejected. He said he met Orsini at Troutt's old nightclub one night when he and his wife went there with the McArthurs. Orsini came by their table, and McArthur introduced her, and he said he never noticed any close relationship between Orsini and McArthur, and that he knew of no marital problems between the McArthurs. Nelson also testified McArthur did not wear a mustache in the summer of 1981.

The prosecution found out about Ms. X and subpoenaed her as a witness. The defense asked that her testimony be given in the judge's chambers, excluding the press, but two reporters challenged the request for a closed hearing, and the judge delayed ruling on it until Monday, after a break for the Thanksgiving holiday. On Monday Judge Hale allowed the news media to listen to the testimony from Ms. X. She testified she had an affair with McArthur in 1975, and the affair ended in 1976 when Alice and the woman's husband found out about it. She said Alice had come to her apartment and was "insistent" on coming inside, and she said she complained about the incident to the prosecuting attorney's office, but no charges were filed against Alice. Ms. X never mentioned the tape-recordings she made of her affair with McArthur or that she had played one of the tapes over the telephone for Alice.

The hearing adjourned for the Thanksgiving holiday.

My conscience is clear on everything I have ever done, the conduct in my personal life and the conduct in my business life—except for an indiscretion—that my conscience is not clear about, but that is the only thing in my life I feel guilty about... I'm not perfect, I have screwed up. I have made mistakes; I have done a lot of different things, but I have never hurt anybody intentionally. It's not fair that my kids are going to have to defend themselves because of accusations made against me.

                                    ... William C. "Bill" McArthur, 1984

Chapter Twenty-Three

ORSINI ARRIVED AT COURT MONDAY LOOK-
ing entirely different from the demure, quiet, dignified
woman she appeared to be before Thanksgiving, when
she dressed in muted colors and wore her hair in a
bun. Now her hair hung loose about her shoulders,
and she wore a white blouse with big ruffles down the
front and a red jacket and skirt. She gave curt answers
and spoke in a louder voice. Before the holiday Orsini's answers were always well thought out and her
voice maintained a level, quiet grace. This time she
seemed eager to answer questions for Dillahunty.

On the day Orsini wore her red outfit, Esther White
Putman, one of McArthur's lawyers, overheard someone at the prosecutor's table tell Dillahunty, "She will
testify to anything now."

Dillahunty drew testimony from Orsini about a
meeting she claimed she had with McArthur in January 1982 at a Hot Springs motel. She said McArthur
wanted her to take $20,000, which he was carrying in a
paper bag, to Yankee Hall as payment for the contract
on Alice, and she said she refused and left the motel
without spending the night. She also testified she had
met with McArthur several other times for the purpose
of relaying messages to Hall. She said Hall originally
told her about the contract on Alice, and she denied
having an affair with Hall and said she and Hall
weren't even particularly close friends.

Orsini claimed she met Hall at a service station

when he walked past her car and commented that it needed some body work. She said she gave him her phone number and told him to call her about the work. But she could have met him as early as the late '70s during the time she frequented a popular Little Rock nightclub, Don T's, the same club where Hall hung out. During that time, she was seen there in the company of several local thugs, and Hall was there so often freeloading beers that he used the club's phone number whenever people asked how to get in touch with him.

When Holt cross-examined Orsini about obtaining the explosives for the bomb planted under Alice's car, she admitted driving Hall several places because she didn't want Hall driving her car.

"Did you ever make a trip with Yankee to see a gentleman named Mr. Wilson about some dynamite?"

"I carried Mr. Hall several places. I did not know the name of Carl Wilson until Sheriff Robinson told me July 5."

"Let's back up on that, did you make a trip with Yankee Hall to Wilson to get some dynamite, yes or no?"

"That can't be answered yes or no."

"Well, give us your answer then."

"Okay, from what I understand, there was dynamite put in my car, but I did not know it was dynamite."

". . . All right, where else did you drive Yankee Hall around?"

"There were several occasions that he would be in North Little Rock, and he did not have transportation, and he would ask me to pick him up and take him someplace."

"For example?"

"I don't know that I could give you an example."

"You don't have any memory of those places?"

"Not right off the top of my head."

"Well, how many times would you pick him up and take him around?"

"Probably three or four different times."

"Why, he was not a friend, you didn't want him to be seen driving your car, why would you pick him up and take him places?"

"Well, Mr. Holt, obviously, I've let a lot of my friends use me."

"I thought you said he wasn't a friend."

"You are the one that is calling him a friend."

"Well, you just got through saying your friends used you, are you putting him in the category of a friend?"

"No, you're putting him there."

"You heard his testimony in your trial, I'm sure."

"Obviously."

"You heard of his statements of an intimate relationship with you."

"I heard his statements."

"And you're saying that's not true?"

"It's absolutely not true."

"You heard his statements that you made the arrangements for a contract with him for the death of Alice McArthur, didn't you?"

"I heard that."

"Are you saying it's not true?"

She nodded affirmatively.

"But Yankee was not a friend. You had no close relationship with him, yet you are trying to tell the court that this stranger, that you had very little relationship with, would sit down and tell you that he had a contract with Bill McArthur to take his wife's life? Is that what you're trying to tell the judge?"

"Mr. Holt, I could give you enough information that that man has told me about half of the people in this town. You know, if you put twenty people up here that are his friends, he has a habit of running his mouth off about you and bragging."

"And he ran his mouth off about you, didn't he?"

"He certainly did. Before he ever even knew me."

"Before he knew you?"

"That's right."

"And yet, you drove him around and took him places and did all these things for this guy that wasn't a friend, that ran his mouth off about you."

"He wasn't running his mouth off at that time. At least I didn't know about it."

"You just found that out recently? Where were you when he told you of this so-called contract, what were the circumstances for him to tell you?"

"It was after Mrs. McArthur's car was bombed."

"Right after it was bombed?"

"Uh huh."

"Why didn't you go to the authorities and report it . . . Miss Orsini?"

"I went to Bill McArthur."

"Oh, you went to Bill?"

She again nodded.

"You mean, this man says that he had contracted with Bill, 'Bill wants it done,' and you had no concern for Alice McArthur, you just go see Bill?"

"Yes, sir. I had enough concern that I told Phoebe and told Alice herself to change her habits."

"Oh, you told her yourself?"

"That's right."

"Did you say, 'Alice, I have talked to Yankee Hall. He has gotten together with Bill. Bill has got a contract with Yankee to take your life so you had better take care of yourself, old girl?'"

"No, I didn't say that."

". . . So, how did you tell this to Alice?"

"I told her, like I told Phoebe, that I . . . to change her habits and not be by herself."

"Did you talk to Alice by telephone?"

"Uh huh."

"You told her who you were?"

"Uh huh."

"Did you tell her that, 'Hey, I think your husband has gotten with Yankee Hall and gotten a contract on you'?"

"No, I didn't tell her that."

"Did you tell her that there was a contract on her?"

"No."

"What did you tell her?"

"Just exactly what I told you awhile ago."

"I've got a poor memory, what did you tell me?"

"I told Alice to change her habits and not be by herself and if she did something on Tuesday, as a normal pattern, then don't do it on Tuesday, every Tuesday."

"Or what would happen, did you tell her?"

"I didn't say that."

"Oh, you didn't tell her what was going to happen?"

"I didn't know what was going to happen."

". . . Well, didn't you see fit to go see Bill McArthur and say, 'Shame on you, Bill'?"

"I did go talk to Bill."

". . . About the contract?"

"Uh huh."

"About Yankee Hall?"

"Uh huh."

"What did he say?"

"At first he denied it."

"Then, what did he say?"

"Well, the position that I got him in, talking about it, he had no other course but to tell me the truth about it."

"You say he told you the truth about it? What was that?"

"That he had hired Hall to kill Alice."

"He just told you that?"

"Uh huh."

"Why would he tell you? Why would he tell that to you?"

"Bill knew he could trust me."

". . . Why did he know he could trust you?"

"Because of what he had over me."

"What did he have over you?"

Dillahunty objected at this point, and after a discussion Holt again asked the question and Orsini again took the Fifth Amendment. Holt continued:

"If this was confirmed in any way by Bill McArthur, why did you not report this to the police and save a life?"

"I wish I would have."

"Why didn't you?"

"Because of what Bill had told me, what he had over me."

"And what did he have over you?"

She again took the Fifth Amendment, invoking her right not to incriminate herself.

". . . Did you talk to Bill any more?"

"Yes."

"What about?"

"On June 8, the election-day runoff, Bill called me some time that morning at my residence and asked me to come have lunch with him. We went to have lunch, and he and Phoebe and I had lunch over at a rib place. He told me to meet him some time around 2 o'clock in the parking lot of U.S. Pizza Company that day on June the 8th, and he wanted to talk to me. And I did, I met him over there. Drove over there and met him. He used to come to my house about once or twice a week to talk to me prior to the bombing. After the bombing, I would not let him come out to my house. I met him over in the U.S. parking lot and he told me that he needed to talk to me, that it was serious and would I meet him some place, and I told him, 'Yes.'"

She testified McArthur told her he was going to be in Hot Springs, and he asked her to meet him the next day at the Holiday Inn on Lake Hamilton. She said she kept the appointment, but she did not stay overnight.

Under Holt's cross-examination, she said while she was in McArthur's office on July 2 he received a telephone call from Alice and that while Alice was talking to McArthur, the doorbell at the McArthur home rang, and he told his wife to answer the door.

Throughout her testimony Orsini kept referring to McArthur as the impetus for every act she committed, and somehow included his name in almost all her answers. She said she went home after leaving McArthur's office on July 2, and when she got home she received a telephone call from McArthur on her daughter's phone, which did not have a trap on it.

"Bill told me to call Phoebe and to tell her that two black men had come to the front door. And that they were driving a late-model Buick."

"He told you to call Phoebe and tell her that?"

"He suggested I call Phoebe or call someone else so that it could be recorded, and I asked him, 'Why?' and he said, 'Just do it. Time is of the essence.'"

"All right, what did you do?"

"I did."

"You called Phoebe and told her that?"

"Uh huh."

"Did you call anybody else?"

"Uh huh. He told me to call the sheriff's department and report it to . . . he said, 'Specifically, Major Dill.'"

Holt began a new line of questioning:

"Do you have recall of writing a script for him [Burge] to call in to the police department? Do you have that recall?"

"That wasn't a script."

"Did you see some writing on paper in your trial?"

"Yes, sir."

"Was that your handwriting?"

"Yes, sir."

"What was the handwriting?"

"It was notes taken from a telephone conversation."

"What did you do with the notes? Were they your notes?"

"Uh huh."

"Your writing?"

"Uh huh."

"What did you have Mr. Burge do with them?"

"I had him call the sheriff's department and give that to the sheriff's department, that information."

". . . Why did you do that?"

"So that I could have a record of the information. I could not tape the other conversation."

"Where did you get the information that was on those. . . ."

"Primarily from Bill McArthur."

The sheriff was the prosecution's last witness. On the last day of the hearing Robinson announced from the witness stand that Bentley, McArthur and Orsini were suspects in the 1981 slaying of Ron Orsini by hindering prosecution. His remarks made headlines.

I saw two entirely different people testify. I joked and said she was Lee the first three days and that was Sue [after Thanksgiving]. . . . Sue was the name she used with Yankee Hall. The first three days she was nice, the kind of woman you would meet at a tea. That day she was an entirely different person, she was talking in a real flippant voice. I think her personality changed that day. I have not seen the 'Mary' personality. Maybe that's the one Tiffany sees.

. . . Esther White Putman, 1985

Chapter Twenty-Four

IT SEEMED AS IF ROBINSON HAD FINALLY won his battle to bring McArthur to trial. Based on the probable cause hearing, Judge David Hale decided to bind the case over for trial in circuit court.

Hale's decision put the case against McArthur back in Bentley's hands. Bentley said he would not decide whether to prosecute McArthur until he had a chance to review all the evidence, but he said that new evidence had surfaced to justify filing charges in the Ron Orsini homicide. Meanwhile, McArthur's personal life and law practice were a shambles. He didn't have enough money to pay his secretary's salary at times, or the office rent, and clients no longer flocked to his door, and contrary to the popular belief that he was getting rich from Alice's oil leases, the payments stopped shortly before Alice's murder when the wells shut down for repairs. Oil prices started going down about that time, and although Alice's children would have inherited all proceeds from the oil leases, the wells were never reopened.

The press was having a field day. There hadn't been this much excitement since nine black students integrated Little Rock Central High School in 1957. It was a good opportunity not only for the politicians to make names for themselves, but also a great time to sell newspapers and assure good news ratings for local television stations. Television cameras clicked on every time Bentley and Robinson came within 10 feet of each other at the courthouse, reporters hung out in the courthouse coffee shop hoping to pick up morsels of information, and the local radio talk show on station KARN pulled out all the stops in its coverage of the McArthur murder. Robinson was invited as a frequent on-air guest to comment on the case, analyze the crime and report on the effectiveness of the county's criminal justice system.

Callers to the talk show believed McArthur probably had his wife killed, had an affair with Lee Orsini, and that Prosecuting Attorney Dub Bentley was covering up everything because of his friendship with McArthur. Robinson reinforced the rumors, insisting Bentley and McArthur were a part of the "good old boy" group at the courthouse that covered for each other.

In one regard, Robinson was right because Arkansas definitely has a good old boy system, but whether McArthur and Bentley were part of it is debatable. Twenty years of Bentley's legal career had been spent in the Air Force; he hadn't been in the state solidifying friendships and business contacts that are so crucial to becoming a good old boy. As for McArthur, he simply did not have as many connections as Robinson claimed.

McClendon's trial began December 13, and the state sought the death penalty on the capital murder charge. The defense complained that the prosecutor was discriminating against McClendon because he was the only black defendant and the only one for whom the state asked execution. Deputy Prosecutor Piazza said the death penalty was not sought for Yankee Hall because his confession and testimony were exchanged for a life sentence.

In addition to Hall's testimony against McClendon, two of Alice McArthur's neighbors testified for the state. One witness, a 16-year-old neighbor who lived

across the street from the McArthurs, said he saw
McClendon walk hurriedly from the McArthur home
that afternoon.

After two days of testimony, the jury convicted
McClendon of first-degree murder and sentenced him
to 20 years in prison. The sentence was made consecu-
tive to the remainder of a 31½-year sentence he had
been paroled from in 1981 for burglary, grand larceny
and robbery.

On December 30 KARN arranged to have Robinson, Bentley and *Arkansas Democrat* Managing Editor
John Robert Starr on the same program to discuss the
case. The station spent a lot of time promoting the
show, which Starr later referred to as the "Great Lipout."

Robinson answered most of the calls during the
show and repeatedly accused Bentley of covering up
for McArthur. Although Bentley attempted to explain
his position to the audience, Robinson kept hammer-
ing away at him, demanding he recuse himself from
the case and hinting Bentley might be impeached.
Robinson said he would meet the following Monday
with Bentley and "pound" on Bentley's desk until he
decided whether to prosecute Bill McArthur for his
wife's death. He accused Bentley of not having the
guts to prosecute McArthur.

For several weeks Bentley put off a decision, and
Robinson's vitriol over Bentley's inaction was winning
public support. Robinson contended Bentley was protecting McArthur. On January 17, 1983 the sheriff,
contending there was a coverup, asked for a grand jury
investigation into the McArthur and Orsini homicides,
and he said a special prosecutor should be appointed
to investigate the cases.

A few days later, January 24, 1983, Bentley held a
news conference to announce his decision not to
charge Bill McArthur with conspiring to have his wife
killed. At the same time Bentley announced he would

charge Lee Orsini with first-degree murder in the 1981 slaying of her husband, Ron. Two hours after Bentley's news conference Robinson appeared on local television stations criticizing Bentley's decision.

On the same day, Robinson hand-delivered a letter to Circuit Judge John Langston asking the judge to impanel a grand jury and appoint a special prosecutor to investigate McArthur's involvement in his wife's slaying. The letter, dated January 17, read:

"The criminal justice system is facing a crisis of confidence because of the behavior of our prosecuting attorney and his failure to impartially represent the State in the McArthur case. Further, I have advised Mr. Bentley that he is suspected of the offense of hindering an investigation in the Orsini murder. If his status as a suspect in the Orsini matter is insufficient to disqualify him to act, then surely his own recusal in the McArthur case should operate as a bar to his resumption of control over both matters."

Also on January 24, Bentley delivered a letter to Judge Langston defending his position. However, according to what the judge said later, this ten-page letter is what prompted him to impanel a grand jury.

It is highly unusual for a judge to determine there is a need for a grand jury; usually the prosecutor does that, but Judge John Langston wasn't a judge cut from the usual mold. He short-circuited the formality of waiting for the prosecutor to request a grand jury and called one himself.

Newly elected to circuit court, Langston didn't look like a judge once he took off his black robe, but rather like a schoolboy who had gotten into more than his share of mischief. He wore cowboy boots, smoked a Texas-sized stogie and had a raspy voice that helped compensate for his otherwise boyish facial features. One could imagine Langston riding bulls in a rodeo or playing in a rag-tag football game, for he had that type of macho appearance.

The day Langston decided to call a grand jury, a workman was hanging wallpaper in his office, and Langston worked quietly in one corner reading and rereading Bentley's letter and answering numerous telephone calls from members of the press who were anxious to hear his decision. Something about Bentley's letter bothered him. Bentley already had declined to participate in the municipal court phase of the case, and when Judge David Hale bound the case over to circuit court, Bentley dropped the charges, refusing to prosecute McArthur. Bentley repeatedly asserted in his letter that there was not enough evidence to warrant prosecuting McArthur, but he added: "Should you determine that a Grand Jury should be called, I will be happy to present the evidence to it. . . ."

Langston could not help but wonder why Bentley was willing to participate in the grand jury, a secret proceeding, when he had refused to participate in the open proceedings of municipal and circuit court. Langston also was worried about the community's lack of faith in the judiciary. Many people believed Sheriff Robinson's accusations, and there was a widespread feeling in the community the judiciary was protecting McArthur.

In a calm moment in his office after he announced his decision to the press, and everyone had left but the workman, Langston asked the man on the ladder, "What do you think about this business?"

The paperhanger wiped his brow with a rag, looked down at the judge and said, "You did good. I will guarantee you, if it had been me instead of a rich criminal lawyer, I would be standing trial."

On January 30, 1983, Super Bowl Sunday, Mrs. Billie McArthur, Bill McArthur's mother, was watching the football game with her grandchildren at her Little Rock home. Suddenly, on the bottom of the television screen, the news flashed that McArthur had been arrested again. Robyn and Chuck began to cry. When the game was interrupted for live coverage of the arrest, the children saw their father clad in an orange jumpsuit and wearing handcuffs.

McArthur had known that Tommy Robinson would relish the opportunity to arrest him again, but he was astounded by the charges. This time the arrest was for an alleged plot hatched by McArthur to assassinate Robinson. The day before McArthur's arrest, Marty Freeman, a twenty-one-year-old man from Benton, a town twenty-five miles from Little Rock in Saline County, went to Sheriff Doyle Cook of Hot Spring County, which is adjacent to Saline County, and said he had been approached by another man to "do a job on the sheriff" of Pulaski County.

Freeman told Sheriff Cook that Michael Swayze, an unemployed twenty-six-year-old truck driver, had approached him and asked him to kill Sheriff Robinson. Freeman and Swayze were arrested and taken to the Pulaski County Sheriff's Department, where Swayze gave a videotaped statement alleging that McArthur had offered him $500,000 to kill Robinson before the grand jury could convene. Swayze then called McArthur at BJ's in the presence of deputies who taped the call and identified himself as "Mike from Malvern" and told McArthur he wanted to meet with him about a job. McArthur arranged an appointment for 4 p.m. that same day at his club, but McArthur did not show up for the appointment. Robinson had Swayze call McArthur again, and this time Swayze was instructed to ask McArthur about a "contract." McArthur answered, "What? What contract?" and told the caller, "You're crazy."

Swayze told McArthur that they had met in Malvern, which is in Hot Spring County, two days earlier. McArthur said, "No, I was in court all day Thursday here in Little Rock." Swayze insisted he met with

McArthur, but McArthur responded, "Not with me you didn't." McArthur reported the second call to the Little Rock police.

Robinson tried unsuccessfully to reach Prosecuting Attorney Dub Bentley. He finally had a deputy prosecuting attorney come to his office and take videotaped statements from Swayze and Freeman. The deputy prosecutor declined to issue a warrant, saying, "If I do, Dub'll just dismiss it." The deputy prosecutor told Robinson he could keep control of the charge by arresting McArthur on probable cause, and that way, Robinson would not need an arrest warrant.

Bentley and Chief Deputy Prosecutor Lloyd Haynes eventually arrived at Robinson's office, and when the sheriff told Bentley and Haynes about the half-million dollars, Haynes said, "That seems like an awfully high price for that job."

Bentley viewed the videotapes and said no testimony indicated an overt act in his area of jurisdiction. After some quick research, Bentley told Robinson that the proper charge would be criminal solicitation to commit murder, but if it took place, it did so in Hot Spring County, outside his jurisdiction.

Robinson and Bentley argued briefly and Robinson finally cursed Bentley and stomped off down a hallway. Bentley and Haynes left the sheriff's office, but shortly afterward, Deputy Bobby Woodward discovered a statute providing that a conspiracy can be prosecuted in any county in which any part of it took place.

"That means we've got a case in Pulaski County," Robinson said.

Robinson put the case on hold until 10 a.m. the next morning, Sunday, January 30, when he drove the forty-five miles to Malvern to meet with the deputy prosecutor for Hot Spring County. Editor Starr accompanied Robinson and later reported the events in the newspaper: Robinson played the videotapes for the deputy prosecutor, who said the overt act took place in Pulaski County. Robinson asked him to issue a warrant for McArthur's arrest, but the deputy prosecutor refused. Robinson took his prisoners back to Little Rock, and during the trip back, Robinson said, "The buck stops with me. I'm going back to the office and look at those law books one more time. If they still say what they said last night, I'm going to arrest Mr. McArthur with or without a warrant."

About 1 p.m. Robinson told Woodward to pick up McArthur. Woodward went to the McArthur home, but McArthur was not there, and Woodward returned to his office and telephoned the McArthur home. This time he reached McArthur and asked him to report to the sheriff's office. That angered Robinson, who told Woodward, "That won't do. Go pick him up."

Woodward went back to the McArthur home but missed McArthur by a few minutes. By the time he got back to the sheriff's department, McArthur pulled into the parking lot, accompanied by his father, Bryan, and his attorney, Jack Holt.

It seemed as though every reporter in town had read about the Swayze arrest in the Sunday morning *Arkansas Democrat*. Television cameras clicked and newspaper photographers ran toward McArthur to record his second arrest. Several deputies met McArthur as he made his way to the jail and escorted him, giving the impression he was a prisoner being taken into custody, rather than someone who was turning himself in. McArthur was booked at the jail while Robinson held a news conference in his office.

This was the first time McArthur went against Holt's advice. Holt told him to wait for a bond hearing so it would not appear he was receiving special treatment, but McArthur was angry and said, "I'm tired of taking the crap Robinson is dishing out. I'm not going to spend another night in his damn jail. I don't care how it looks. I'm not guilty of anything, and I'm not going to be subjected to any more humiliation just so Robinson can make headlines. Call a judge, and let's have a bond hearing today, right now!"

Holt called Robinson's office from the jail and said Judge Langston was "inclined to put McArthur on a $50,000 recognizance bond."

"I'd be inclined to raise hell if he does," Robinson said. "Tell him to get a writ [of habeas corpus, which is used to bring a prisoner from prison to court in order to testify or to release a prisoner who is being held illegally]. We're ready to go to court."

Ten minutes later Langston called Robinson, who remarked to a newspaper reporter, "Oh, what swift justice one can get if he knows somebody." Langston set a hearing for 4 p.m. that afternoon.

A deputy told Robinson that Holt wanted to know if he could take McArthur to court and if McArthur could wear his own clothes, two requests which were not unusual. Many prisoners were allowed to appear in street clothes, but Robinson would not allow it. McArthur's televised appearance in an orange jumpsuit, white tennis shoes and handcuffs came during the first half of the game between the Washington Redskins and the Miami Dolphins.

When McArthur entered the courtroom for his bond hearing at 4:13 p.m., Dub Bentley was present. Bentley told the court he had advised Robinson the night before he did not have sufficient evidence to establish that an overt act in a murder conspiracy had been committed in Pulaski County.

Robinson asked if he could present the evidence himself, and the judge allowed him to show his videotapes. Then Robinson called the judge's attention to Arkansas Statute 43-1414 discovered by Woodward on Saturday.

Holt, McArthur's attorney, took the witness stand

and said he was with McArthur between 12:25 and 1:00 p.m. on the day Swayze said he met McArthur in Malvern. Judges, lawyers and several reporters later stated that they, too, had seen McArthur at the courthouse during the time period Swayze claimed to have met with him. McArthur took the stand and explained he had agreed to meet with the telephone caller because, "I was trying to get rid of him, really," McArthur said.

Langston set a bond of $50,000, and three of McArthur's friends posted it. As he left the courtroom, Robinson told reporters, "The state didn't represent me today. The state represented the defense."

McArthur called a news conference on Monday to say he had no connection with Swayze. "I think it would take an absolute idiot to do what I'm charged with," he said. "I would not ask any harm come to Sheriff Robinson. I want to expose the man for what he is."

He then said Lee Orsini's testimony against him at his probable cause hearing had relieved him of any obligation under the attorney/client privilege, and he said he was now certain she had murdered her husband in 1981.

Robinson was talking to reporters on Monday, too. He told the media that cocaine trafficking was a common thread in the Orsini murder and the McArthur murder.

On Tuesday morning, at McArthur's conspiracy charge arraignment in Pulaski County Municipal Court before Judge Hale, Holt cited Robinson's remark about cocaine trafficking and asked Judge Hale for a ban against any public discussion of the case by the principals, and Judge Hale imposed a gag order. Afterward Robinson told reporters, "Something stinks in our judicial system, but I'm going to do something about it, even if I get some of the smell on myself."

On Wednesday Swayze and Freeman went before

Judge Hale for arraignment. Instead of being returned to Robinson's custody, Hale ordered the state police to deliver Swayze and Freeman to the Little Rock Police Department jail. Swayze's lawyer, a public defender, told Bentley that Swayze had changed his story, and Bentley came to the jail to take another statement from Swayze. Later that afternoon, Swayze repeated his statement at a bond hearing for himself and Freeman.

Swayze testified the death plot was "all a stupid, lousy joke." He said he tried to tell Robinson, but the sheriff did not believe him. In fact, the sheriff accused Bentley of pressuring Swayze to change his statement.

Later that week, Robinson addressed a noon meeting of the Pulaski Visitors Council and reminded his audience he was under Judge Hale's gag order, but added, "They might put me in jail, then I can run my mouth in jail . . . and the only thing they can do then is [physically] gag me."

He criticized the witnesses who said they saw McArthur at the courthouse during the time he was supposedly meeting with Swayze:

"How many times do you go somewhere and say, 'Oh my God, I better write down the time, it's thirty seconds past so and so. I just saw that person over there, and if they get arrested in three days, I better come up and write that down where I can be an alibi.' That's bull manure," Robinson said.

Later in the day, Robinson called a news conference for 7 p.m. and admitted that he was deliberately violating the gag order. During the news conference, he played some of the videotaped and tape-recorded evidence for the media and accused Bentley of making a deal with Swayze. Robinson's widely reported allegations against McArthur and his criticism of Bentley increased the public's suspicion that McArthur had something to hide, and powerful and influential people were protecting him.

The next morning, Holt and Bentley asked Hale to hold Robinson in contempt for violating the gag order. Hale cited both Robinson and Major Dill for criminal and civil contempt, but he did not send them to jail.

The next day Judge Hale released Freeman and bound Swayze over for trial in circuit court with the admonition that no one was laughing at his "stupid, lousy joke." That move put the Swayze case in Bentley's hands, and on February 14 Bentley charged Swayze with perjury and said he could not in "good conscience" prosecute Swayze in the alleged conspiracy. That same day, Orsini declined to enter a plea to the charge of killing her husband, so Circuit Court Judge Langston entered an innocent plea on her behalf. A jury trial was scheduled for her for later that year, and by the time Orsini came to trial in the fall of 1983 for the murder of her husband, more than two years had passed since the 1981 grand jury returned no indictments in the investigation of Ron Orsini's death.

On February 2, 1983, McArthur filed a civil rights lawsuit in federal court against Robinson and Dill claiming false arrest and malicious prosecution. The suit charged Dill with conspiring with the sheriff to deprive McArthur of his constitutional rights. It claimed Robinson fabricated charges in both arrests and acted with malice in his investigations of McArthur and said the sheriff waged an extensive media campaign which created a climate that made it impossible for McArthur to get a fair trial. The suit accused Robinson of using media tactics of verbal attacks on lawyers, judges and prosecuting attorneys who disagreed with him. The suit said Robinson made several statements to the media claiming that he was holding back additional evidence in the case, and that each time Robinson arrested McArthur he notified the media to ensure that

McArthur was photographed while in custody. The suit also said McArthur had suffered loss of income from his private law practice as a result of the sheriff's actions.

Responding to the suit, Robinson told reporters, "If he's so broke now, how come he has seven lawyers and a honky tonk?"

I am as sincere as I can be when I say I do not believe Bill McArthur was involved with the death of his wife. However, whether he was or wasn't, the evidence never was there to warrant charging him with the murder of his wife, and it would have been unethical to succumb to the pressure that was put on me and subject that man to a trial when the evidence wasn't sufficient.

... Wilbur C. "Dub" Bentley, 1984

Chapter Twenty-Five

RIGHT AFTER THE SWAYZE CASE MADE headlines, Judge John Langston set out to find an attorney who would be willing to serve as special prosecutor and present evidence to the grand jury in its investigation of Bill McArthur. Since McArthur had been practicing law in Little Rock for 14 years, it was difficult to find a lawyer who had not had any past dealings with him.

Langston eventually approached Darrell F. Brown with the job. Brown was a lean, athletic-looking, thirty-four-year-old who had attended the University of Arkansas School of Law on a grant from the Carnegie Foundation, was a leader in college in the Black Americans for Democracy, and had served as federal magistrate for the Cristoba District of Panama from 1972 to 1979. Brown was recommended for that post the year he graduated from law school by the late U.S. Senator John L. McClellan. Brown returned to Little Rock from Panama in 1979 to open a private law practice.

Langston instructed Brown to talk to all the parties involved, including Bentley and Robinson, and determine whether they objected to his appointment as special prosecutor. Bentley and McArthur's lawyers had no objection, and when Brown went to Robinson, the sheriff told him he knew Langston was considering appointing him and he had already checked out Brown.

He said he thought Brown was a fine man for the job. Brown accepted the appointment.

Shortly after the grand jury convened in February, 1983, Brown became concerned about electronic surveillance. His curiosity first became aroused when he began hearing things repeated to him by Sheriff Robinson and Major Dill he knew had only just come up before the grand jury, sometimes on the same day.

Brown realized many people wanted to know what was going on inside the grand jury, and many people could be suspected of eavesdropping on the proceedings. He also did not rule out the possibility the leak might be coming from inside, from a juror or court official.

During the nine-week grand jury session, Brown's concerns intensified, and he contacted the state police about the matter. They identified several experts on wiretapping and electronic surveillance, and one of them happened to be employed at the sheriff's department. He also learned that after Robinson took office, the sheriff's department had purchased some very sophisticated electronic surveillance equipment. Brown examined the telephone box at the rear of his home and found that someone had tampered with it. Brown then had the state police check the grand jury room for bugging devices, and although there was evidence a bug had been there, no bugs were found.

When Robinson learned Brown was getting the cooperation of the state police, he called Brown and told him he had heard the state police were "snooping" around and he thought that was a mistake. Then Robinson offered to investigate the bugging himself. Trying to be noncommittal, Brown told him, "Just let me know what you find, and we'll go from there." Looking back, Brown said he believed electronic surveillance occurred and that it might have been a law enforcement agency, but he said he couldn't link it to the sheriff's office or Robinson.

Throughout the grand jury proceedings Robinson dropped by Brown's office every day after the jury recessed. He called Brown's office every evening and in the mornings before the grand jury resumed and sometimes showed up when they broke for lunch. He also gave Brown a badge and a deputy's card and a gun, which Brown put in a box of clothes for safekeeping, and he offered to let Brown use county credit cards for gasoline purchases, but Brown declined.

Several grand jurors began reporting they were getting annoying calls at home, and some suspected their phone lines were bugged. A few reported seeing sheriff's patrol cars in their neighborhoods. As the grand jury delved deeper into the case, Brown saw some of the jurors become increasingly paranoid. Part of this paranoia could be discounted, he felt, because these "average" citizens were dealing with a notorious murder case, but Brown was becoming increasingly concerned.

When Brown began receiving threats himself, he realized someone was playing hardball. Not only did he receive threatening phone calls, but at one point he received a report from the LRPD that they had information his life was in danger.

Brown had to decide if he was willing to risk his own safety—and perhaps that of his family—in order to maintain the confidentiality and impartiality of the grand jury. Was the commitment he made to Judge Langston to conduct the proceedings impartially worth such a personal sacrifice, or should he step aside and avoid any possible danger? He resolved to take his chances. Even if he did get hurt, he was going to con-

duct an impartial investigation. Brown was, above all,
a believer in the system.

The problems didn't stop with apparent wiretapping.
Brown's office was broken into at least once during the
McArthur grand jury. The first time was on the second
night of the proceedings. After the janitor and maid
left his office in the Union Bank Building in downtown
Little Rock, Brown placed all files but one pertaining
to the investigation on the floor and locked his office
door. He taped the top of the door from the outside,
as he had seen done in detective movies. The next
morning the tape was broken and three files were on
his desk instead of one.

One of Brown's biggest concerns during the grand
jury investigation was the credibility of Robinson's
witnesses. Many of them seemed to expect something
in return for their testimony. One witness, who died
not long after the grand jury completed its investigation, was physically ill while he was questioned at the
sheriff's office. The man had just been released from
the hospital and was on medication, but he was questioned for more than six hours.

Brown saw clearly from the beginning that Robinson
was obsessed with getting Bill McArthur. Some of the
things Robinson said to Brown concerned him so much
he had the state police install hidden videotape equipment in his office to record Robinson's visits.

Brown said that many times Robinson asked, "Do
you think we are going to get him?"

Brown would reply, "It depends on the evidence. It's
interesting. Some of this stuff I don't believe."

Toward the end of the grand jury proceedings Robinson became impatient and told Brown he should give
the jurors the "dynamite jury instructions," which
meant if there is a deadlock, the jurors are told they
must return a verdict. Obviously, Robinson did not

know these instructions are only given in court trials, never to grand juries. Robinson's impatience soon turned to desperation.

Brown said Robinson told him, "You have got to reach a verdict; you have to find the son-of-a-bitch guilty. You have got to get this jury to indict Bill McArthur. If you don't, they will have my ass and your ass, too."

Brown said Robinson told him they would both have good futures if Bill McArthur was indicted, but if McArthur wasn't indicted, it would mean the end of Robinson's political career. Brown said the sheriff also told him, "If you get Bill McArthur, the doors are going to swing wide open. Everybody will eat cheese, the judges will eat cheese because I was the one who was right."

"Even if you don't get an indictment, you have done your job," Brown told Robinson.

Brown said Robinson agreed with him but stressed how important it was to see McArthur indicted. When Brown asked if it was all that important, he said Robinson told him "You're damn right it is. One of these days I'll be somebody more than sheriff. I won't be sheriff all my life."

The sheriff's perception of right is wrong. His thought process is warped.... He even said, 'Regardless of whether the SOB is found guilty, he is going to jail.' And that's scary! Every time I hear Tommy Robinson's name called, a flag pops up in my mind. It gives me an appreciation for what the flag is supposed to be; and then it creates frustration—when I know what he has done to that flag—I am not talking about his approach to me, I can deal with that—but his total disregard for the rights of those persons he causes to come into the system.

...Darrell F. Brown, 1984

Chapter Twenty-Six

ON THE DAY LEE ORSINI TESTIFIED BEFORE the grand jury, Brown said Robinson told him, "The bitch is going to lie. [But] the only thing she'll lie about is she didn't have anything to do with it. She had something to do with it, but she shouldn't have life, not if Bill McArthur is walking around on the street."

After each time she testified, Orsini would question Brown, looking for his approval as he escorted her out of the grand jury room: "How did I do, do you think they are going to get Bill?"

And each time he would tell her: "I can't talk to you out of the presence of your attorneys."

While the grand jury testimony is secret—and remains sealed indefinitely—interviews with several key people involved in the investigation reveal several major areas of confusion involving conflicting testimony from the Little Rock Police Department and the Pulaski County Sheriff's Department about events at the crime scene the day of Alice McArthur's death.

The grand jury knew the LRPD had received a tip about a contract on Alice McArthur's life, and they thought the sheriff's department might have received similar information. The jury also had gotten a tip that someone from the sheriff's office was on stakeout at the McArthur home the day Alice was killed. Stan Brown, the foreman of the grand jury, later explained that the grand jury investigated the possibility Captain Bobby Woodward might have been the one on stakeout. If he was nearby or arrived shortly after the homicide occurred, he might know something about the flowers.

Woodward, who was later convicted of criminal conspiracy in connection with a "sting" operation, denied he was present at the McArthur home the afternoon of Alice's murder, and members of the sheriff's department, including Major Larry Dill, who were present at the McArthur home immediately after Mrs. McArthur's body was found, testified Woodward was not there that day, but a Little Rock police officer testified differently, and one sheriff's deputy testified he "thought" Woodward was there but was not positive.

The first officer on the scene was Officer Robert McNeely of the LRPD. Shortly after NcNeely's arrival, Major Dill of the sheriff's office and Officer Rick Edgar of the LRPD arrived and assisted McNeely in securing the crime scene, and within minutes several sheriff's deputies arrived. Edgar told the grand jurors that he saw Woodward leaning over, looking into the closet and Edgar said Woodward told him he was looking for flowers, although the significance of the flowers had not yet been established.

The grand jurors weren't the only ones concerned with Woodward's whereabouts on July 2. Lee Orsini seemed preoccupied with the question during a prison interview more than a year later. Without prompting she brought up the subject of Woodward's whereabouts and said she was at Tommy Robinson's office when Woodward arrived the afternoon of July 2, "with a case of beer under his arm." She said Woodward had learned of Alice's murder from a radio in the liquor store and rushed directly to the sheriff's department. She didn't explain, however, why he still had the beer with him.

Conflicting grand jury testimony also was given regarding the flower arrangement found at Mrs. McArthur's feet. Officers McNeely and Edgar said they did not notice it when they looked into the closet, but it shows up in the crime scene photos taken later. Major Dill reported seeing flower petals in the hall, but the two Little Rock policemen said they saw no such thing, and Hall testified McClendon told him Mrs. McArthur dropped the flowers while running away. Robinson later contended that McArthur moved the flowers from where they had been dropped and placed them at her feet before calling the police.

Another strange piece of evidence which perplexed the grand jury was a partial dental plate which was discovered in the closet by Alice's friends as they were cleaning the house a week or so after the murder. Neither Alice nor McArthur wore bridgework, and although the prosecutor's office attempted to locate the owner, the dental plate still remains a mystery.

A radio transmission made by members of the sheriff's office on July 2, 1982, was, perhaps, the most unsettling piece of evidence heard by the grand jurors. The radio communications of the sheriff's department are recorded on a slow-moving 24-hour tape. Judge Langston, who impaneled the grand jury, heard about the existence of this particular transmission, which was evidently overheard by several deputies. The judge sent his bailiff, Les Gachot, to the sheriff's department with instructions to listen to the part of the tape recorded the afternoon of July 2.

Gachot had the kind of imposing physical appearance which made him an unlikely person to be refused anything. Once a Little Rock policeman, Gachot tipped the scales well over 200 pounds, with the broad shoulders of a middle linebacker. When he presented himself at the sheriff's office and announced he was there at the behest of Judge Langston, the deputy on duty quickly accommodated him and played the tape for him. While Gachot listened to the tape, Sheriff Robinson came in and expressed outrage Gachot had been allowed access to it. Gachot left but carried the twenty-four hour reel of tape back with him to Langston's office.

Upon returning to the courthouse, Gachot and the judge locked the tape safely away in the judge's safe until it could be played for the grand jury. The next day there was a bomb scare at the courthouse, and, according to Langston, his office was the first one converged upon by sheriff's deputies who were trying to clear everyone out of the building. Gachot didn't take any chances—he took the tape with him. Langston said he never listened to this tape because it was a part of the grand jury evidence, and it remains locked away in his safe. Later it was played for the grand jurors—a moment they all will surely remember the remainder of their days.

First deputy: "We've got one down at the McArthur house."

Second deputy: "One of ours or one of theirs?" Then, when the second deputy was told who had been killed, there was the sound of laughter.

I heard rumors that Woodward was supposed to be in the house, but he wasn't even at the scene. The radio tapes back that up. . . . There was a rumor that we had a stakeout. They were hell bent to putting Woodward and Robinson out there on a stakeout, and me too, but they couldn't figure out how McArthur could call me here [at headquarters] if I were on stakeout.

. . . Major Larry Dill, 1985
Pulaski County Sheriff's Department

Chapter Twenty-Seven

BILL MCARTHUR'S ATTORNEY, JACK HOLT, was glad the case had been turned over to a grand jury because he felt it was a good way of protecting unfairly accused people from the publicity of a trial, and he believed everyone was entitled to a certain amount of privacy.

Although the jurors could have been called "pro-Robinson" in the beginning, they learned throughout the investigation that they couldn't believe all the witnesses provided by Robinson's office. Almost all of what the sheriff considered evidence came from Lee Orsini, with very little corroboration from other witnesses, according to Special Prosecutor Brown, who found that everything tied back to her. Brown believed Robinson sincerely thought McArthur was guilty, but he thought some of Robinson's tactics were questionable.

While the jurors were not able to resolve the whereabouts of Bobby Woodward on July 2 or the mystery of whether Alice carried the flowers with her as she ran into the closet, they suspected that several law enforcement agencies, including the sheriff's office, had prior knowledge a "salt-and-pepper" team would try to kill Alice on July 2. The grand jury tried to run down Bob Troutt's allegation that he called the LRPD with the information but could not determine whether Troutt's allegation was true. Later, however, in an interview for this book, then Little Rock Assistant Police Chief Doc Hale confirmed Troutt's story but said he did not know what went wrong once Troutt's tip was received by the LRPD.

Copies of documents obtained later through the Arkansas Freedom of Information Act from the Little Rock Police Department backed up Troutt's allegation and proved that not only did the Little Rock police have reason to believe an attempt would be made on Alice's life, but so did the state police and the Bureau of Alcohol, Tobacco and Firearms. A nine-page ATF report carries the following notation, date 7/2/82, 4 p.m.:

"The LRPD Intelligence Unit gave Agent Spurgeon a copy of a memo which said that Bob Troutt called the Arkansas State Police on 7/1/82 and said a white male named 'Chuck' was in town with a 9mm pistol and possibly had a 'contract' to kill Alice McArthur."

Regarding the possibility of illegal wiretapping of the grand jury, Foreman Stan Brown said he didn't know for certain if it actually occurred, but he recalled a conversation in Judge Langston's office among himself, Darrell Brown and the judge that appeared in a newspaper the next morning.

In the end the consensus of opinion among the grand jurors was that Bill McArthur was a victim, as much a victim as his wife, and on April 28, 1983, they announced they would not indict him.

Bill McArthur didn't have much time to mourn Alice. He was too busy fighting for his reputation, his career, his children and their future to allow time to grieve. The most difficult part was understanding the motive behind Lee Orsini's behavior, and he came to believe she had manipulated him from the beginning.

But why? McArthur asked himself. Was Orsini in love with him? Did she intend to frame him for

Alice's murder? Did she want to get caught? Was anyone else involved in the slaying? No one will ever be certain.

One thing is certain. If a visitor to Arkansas mentions Bill McArthur's name in a country store, roadside service station or just about any other place, he's likely to be told, "That's the man who killed his wife." One of the most ironic aspects of this story is that a man who was vindicated by a lengthy grand jury investigation remains guilty in the eyes of many of the public. It's not hard to understand why: publicity, the publicity primarily generated by Sheriff Robinson. Throughout the fall of 1982 Robinson voiced his theories about Bill and Alice McArthur at every opportunity, sometimes in violation of court order. Some members of the sheriff's office even spread rumors that Alice was a lesbian, and when Robinson spoke to the Pocahontas, Arkansas, Rotary Club at its weekly luncheon meeting in August 1983, in answer to a question from the audience, "Is William McArthur guilty?" Robinson responded, "Is the Pope a Catholic?"

Then Robinson added, "I'm sick and tired of the McArthur case. McArthur is guilty, but he may never be convicted. . . ."

Robinson was finally silenced when an out-of-court settlement was reached in 1983 in McArthur's civil rights lawsuit against him. One of the agreements of the settlement was that Robinson and Dill would cease accusing him of any complicity in Alice's death, and McArthur would cease accusing Robinson of false arrest. The monetary amount of the settlement was not disclosed, but it was rumored McArthur was paid about $100,000 by the insurance company representing the Pulaski County Sheriff's Office. McArthur would have had to pay his attorneys out of that amount before realizing any money himself and by that time, he owed Jack Holt $50,000 in legal fees.

THE COPS

Jess F. "Doc" Hale retired from the Little Rock Police Department and went to work for the state Attorney General's office. Then in 1986 he got back into law enforcement when he was named Little Rock chief of police.

Fred Hensley, the detective who said he overheard Lee Orsini's attorney tell Sheriff Robinson, "Lee will do whatever we tell her to do," stayed with the LRPD. Al Dawson stayed on the police force too, as did Robert McNeeley, but Rick Edgar, the officer who told the grand jury he saw Bobby Woodward at the McArthur home the afternoon of July 2, quit the police department to sell real estate.

Forrest Parkman, the former LRPD detective who interviewed Yankee Hall, died on Wednesday, June 6, 1984, at the age of fifty-one from complications following a heart attack.

Officer Mike Willingham left the LRPD and moved out of state. His friends said he later took a job as a bodyguard for country singer Willie Nelson, but he was later convicted in Arkansas of mail fraud in connection with arson and sentenced to three years in federal prison in July, 1987.

Jim Lester, who was hired by McArthur as a private investigator during the 1981 grand jury investigation into the murder of Ron Orsini, went back to work for the Arkansas State Police.

Major Larry Dill stayed at the sheriff's office under a

new sheriff but considered going back to school and possibly becoming a high school coach.

Pulaski County sheriff's deputy Bobby Woodward was found guilty of criminal conspiracy to commit burglary and theft in connection with a sting operation and sentenced by Judge John Langston to three years in prison and fined $10,000.

Tommy Robinson's career as sheriff ended with Bob Troutt's case being the only conviction of all the highly publicized arrests he made while sheriff. Largely as a result of the media attentions he received while sheriff, Robinson was elected to the United States House of Representatives in 1984 and in 1986 was picked by his fellow Democrat freshmen to serve as whip for the new Democrat House members. He declined an interview for this book, and one of his aides said Robinson wanted to forget the McArthur case ever happened.

THE LAWYERS

Pulaski County Prosecuting Attorney Wilbur "Dub" Bentley made a bid for the Arkansas Supreme Court in 1984 but was soundly defeated. He went into private law practice.

Deputy prosecuting Attorney Chris Piazza was elected Pulaski County Prosecuting Attorney and took office on January 1, 1985.

Jack Holt, the attorney who represented McArthur during his November 1982 probable cause hearing, was elected to the Arkansas Supreme Court and took office as chief justice in January 1985.

Jack Lessenberry, Orsini's attorney during her trial for Alice's murder, was elected as a Pulaski County Circuit Court judge in 1984 and took office in 1985. Tom Donovan, Orsini's second attorney, moved his law practice from Dardanelle to North Little Rock.

In June 1985, the Arkansas Supreme Court ruled that the county would not have to pay Darrell Brown's bill of $81,000 because the judge had no authority to appoint him to serve as special prosecutor for the 1983 Pulaski County Grand Jury. The court said Pulaski County Circuit Judge John Langston had overstepped his authority when he appointed Brown and that a circuit judge may only appoint a special prosecutor when the incumbent county prosecutor is being investigated for or has been charged with criminal activity. Brown is currently practicing law in Little Rock, and when interviewed for this book, he talked about the likelihood of McArthur's involvement in Alice's murder: "If Bill McArthur planned all this, he has to be the worst planner I have ever run into. It was stupid. If you plan at all, you have to know that a death in the family will do a lot to the surrounding family, the immediate family, his career, the fear and anguish, but the question always comes back around, 'Why Alice McArthur?'"

The bill for Sonny Dillahunty's work as special prosecutor during McArthur's November 1982 probable cause hearing also went unpaid. The Arkansas Supreme Court ruled that since Municipal Judge David Hale had no authority to appoint Dillahunty, Pulaski County was not responsible for Dillahunty's $16,125 bill for services.

Dillahunty believed McArthur was guilty of having something to do with Alice's murder long after the grand jury ended. His reasons were manifold:

• He did not believe Alice would have opened the door to a stranger, especially a black man.

• He thought McArthur should have noticed the damage to the grasscloth in the hallway on his first trip down the hall.

• Despite Anita Prather's testimony to the contrary, he thought McArthur summoned her to his home on July 2 so she could find the body: "Somebody else has got to find the body, that's the most important damn thing in this whole case. That person has to stand the interrogation....," Dillahunty said when interviewed later.

• Dillahunty also said he was not sure whether Larry McClendon was the one who pulled the trigger, and he doubted Alice was shot inside the closet.

"The scenario has got to be one of two ways," Dillahunty said. "He [McClendon] hands her the flowers, and he pulls the gun, takes a shot at her, and she holds on to the flowers, runs up those steps still holding the flowers while he's chasing her with a gun, and she goes on into the bedroom after getting around that ironing board somehow...or would you think the lady probably would have hauled off and thrown the damn flowers at somebody and run like hell? Then you've got to go back to the other scenario, does he keep the flowers in his hand and have the gun in the other hand, and he's chasing her holding the flowers and shooting at her, making sure he's got the flowers when he got up there? So, then, how did the flowers get between her feet? Somebody picked them up and put them there...the flowers are handed to her, [then] set down to sign something, then all of a sudden, hell broke loose. I can't figure out in my mind why the flowers would ever go up there to begin with. It doesn't make sense...I have a funny feeling about those flowers...."

THE WITNESSES AND BIT PLAYERS

Dr. Charles Wulz continued the practice of veterinary medicine in Sherwood, a small community near North Little Rock. He visits Orsini at the women's prison every other Sunday and said he pays the rent on Mrs. Hatcher's apartment each month out of his own pocket.

Bob Troutt was convicted in April 1983, of first-degree battery as a result of the beating of disc jockey Bob Robbins and sentenced to twelve years in prison and fined $15,000. His nightclub went out of business, and after serving nine months in an Arkansas prison, Troutt was released on a work release program on July 26, 1985. He met with the parole board in August 1986 but was denied parole, and he is due to complete his sentence on October 20, 1990 unless he is paroled earlier.

Ron Orsini's sister, Linda House, said their family wants to be left alone. She said the family is bitter over some of the publicity generated by her brother's murder, especially the attempt by Lee Orsini to make people believe her brother was involved in drugs. She said her brother deserves to rest in peace, and she thinks that's what he is doing.

Phoebe Jones Pinkston remained loyal to McArthur throughout the investigation and still works for him. It took her a long time to get over feeling guilty for telling Orsini so many things about her boss and his wife, especially about the children being away at camp.

THE KILLERS

Larry McClendon's twenty-year sentence for slaying Alice McArthur was added to the remainder of another sentence he had been paroled from in July 1981, making his total sentence fifty-one years, six months. Due to court rulings affecting sentencing in Arkansas, McClendon became eligible for parole in 1985 but was denied parole in August 1985, 1986 and 1987. Each August McClendon appears before the parole board hoping for a chance at freedom.

* * *

Yankee Hall is serving a life sentence in the Arkansas Department of Correction, where he works as a prison barber. He is not eligible for parole. In a 1984 prison interview he recanted his confession regarding Alice's murder, saying that the only reason his fingerprints were on the flowers was because Orsini had asked him to buy flowers for her to give to Tiffany. He said he left the flowers on the doorstep of his house for Orsini to pick up later, and Orsini took them to the murder scene.

It is entirely possible that Hall, not McClendon, pulled the trigger and murdered Alice. Hall admits going into the house after McClendon. What if Hall heard the first shot—and a pause—and became worried that something was wrong, so he went into the house to check things out and heard McClendon upstairs looking for Alice, who was hiding in the closet? Hall might have followed them upstairs, noticed the flowers where Alice dropped them, picked them up and walked into the bedroom. This scenario could have taken only seconds to unfold, and in the interim, McClendon could have taken his second shot at Alice —the bullet missing her again. Hall might have set the flowers down, grabbed the gun away from McClendon, who was probably unnerved at having missed Alice twice, and taken matters into his own hands. Then, in his haste to get away, Hall forgot the flowers and ran out of the house with McClendon.

This chain of events would explain why Hall was so anxious to plea bargain. He knew he actually pulled the trigger, his prints were on the vase, and he might get the electric chair if convicted for capital murder, so he tried to get himself a life sentence. It would also explain how the flowers ended up at Alice's feet but not the conflicting grand jury testimony concerning the flowers.

Mary Lee Orsini was convicted in November 1983, for the March 11, 1981 slaying of her husband, Ron. She was sentenced to life in prison without parole, which gave her two life sentences. In an interview for this book, the state medical examiner, Dr. Malak, said Orsini tried to obtain arsenic from him prior to Alice McArthur's murder. She had gone to see him to discuss her husband's death and told him she needed some arsenic so she could kill rodents around her house, but Malak did not give it to her.

The Arkansas Supreme Court on June 17, 1985, overturned the murder conviction in her husband's death because of faulty jury instructions. The high court said Judge Langston should not have given instructions about the possibility that she was an accomplice in the death of her husband. The instructions permitted the state to maintain simultaneously that she killed her husband because no one else could have done it, and that if someone else killed him, she must have participated in the crime. The court rejected her contention that the evidence did not support her conviction. Newly elected Pulaski County Prosecuting Attorney Chris Piazza refused to retry her in that case because she was already serving a life sentence for Alice's murder.

Orsini's conviction in Alice's slaying was upheld by the state Supreme Court, and she is currently in the early stages of her last avenue of appeal at the federal level. Attorney Clint Miller of the state Attorney General's office, who is representing the state in federal court regarding Orsini's appeal process, does not believe anything in her case will warrant review by the United States Supreme Court. Provided her appeals to federal court are unsuccessful, she'll remain in prison the rest of her life, unless she receives a gubernatorial pardon.

THE VICTIMS

McArthur and Lassiter dissolved their law partnership, and McArthur set up a small office in downtown Little

Rock. He gave his children the choice of selling their home at 24 Inverness and making a new start, but they chose to remain in the home they had shared with Alice and did so until the summer of 1987. At that time McArthur, who had remarried after Alice's death, divorced and remarried again, sold the home for $185,000 and moved to a house on ten acres of land about fifteen miles west of Little Rock.

Tiffany Orsini lived with her grandmother, Julia Hatcher, until she married in 1986, a few months prior to her graduation from high school. She doesn't visit her mother very often. She told her uncle, Ron Hatcher, it depressed her to go to the prison, but Mrs. Hatcher and Orsini's sister, Frances, visit her regularly.

Ron Hatcher was an executive with a Little Rock bank until he took his own life with a .38-caliber pistol in January 1987. About a year before his death, he said as far as he was concerned, the state prison was his sister's home, and that's the way he thought it should be. He said he had no compassion, no love, no feeling for her at all, only a sense of satisfaction that she got what she deserved—finally.

I wish I could change people's minds, . . . but there are a certain number of people that would believe me guilty no matter what I did. A certain number of those people, even if Christ came down and manifested himself in Little Rock, Arkansas, today and announced that Bill McArthur is innocent, they would not believe him.

You know, you have always heard that 'beauty is skin deep, but ugly is all the way to the bone.' Well, ignorance is too, and I am not talking about education because I know a lot of people who are quite well educated who are ignorant as hell—little minds draw conclusions and never change, regardless. I don't want to waste my time and effort, whatever they want to be-

lieve, I don't give a damn, but I don't want my kids aggravated by it. If anybody ever comes up to them and says, 'Your father is a murderer,' they better not have me standing nearby because they will regret they ever said that. . . .

People stare constantly. I try not to embarrass them when they stare; I usually speak to them. It doesn't bother the kids. They have never had any doubt about me. I have never lied to them about anything, and they know that. Early on in this, any questions they had I answered, whether they made me look good or bad, and they believe me and know me. They know I'm gentle, a pacifist. I hate to spank them, they know that. I am one of those parents who it actually does hurt me more than it does them. I have done it, but they know it bothers me to have to spank them.

Both of my children are very protective of my feelings and have been for the last couple of years. They are careful about what they say, especially in talking about Alice. We always have talked about Alice. We go to the cemetery. I go more by myself than with them. . . . The first time I went, I told them I was going out there occasionally, and if they ever wanted to go with me, they were welcome, but it was strictly up to them. Finally, one day they told me they wanted to go so we went out, and when we got there, I said, 'You know, of course, your mother's not here. This is merely a symbol. This is where her physical body is buried, and you don't have to come here to talk to her. You can talk to her anywhere you want to, at home or school or anywhere.' They understood that and have only asked to go back out there one other time.

. . . William C. "Bill" McArthur, 1984

INDEX

Agent Spurgeon, 216
Alcohol Beverage Control Board, 56
Bureau of Alcohol, Tobacco and Firearms, 55, 78, 100, 133, 216
"Allen, John," 2, 6, 159
Arkansas Associated Press Broadcasters' Association, 130
Arkansas Democrat, 15, 61, 100, 120, 122–23, 134, 136, 152, 168, 195, 200
Arkansas Department of Correction, 223
Arkansas Gazette, 61, 100, 122–23, 135, 136, 178
Arkansas Razorbacks, 68, 71
Arkansas Repertory Theatre, 170
Arkansas State Police, 38, 216, 218
Arkansas Supreme Court, 220
  overturns murder conviction, 224
Arkansas Tech University, 45
Arsenic, 224
Assassination plot, 198–99, 203
Attorney/client privilege, 202

Bahamas, 29
Bailey, F. Lee, 40
Bass, Mary, 4, 5
Baton Rouge, Louisiana, 73
Bayou LaFourche, 23
Beer, 212
Bentley, Wilbur C. "Dub," 36–37, 80, 108, 126, 150, 152, 153, 176, 178, 182, 192, 193, 195–96, 199, 201, 203, 205, 219
  announces plans to seek death penalty, 129
  criticized in editorial, 130
  subpoenas sheriff's files, 128
  withdraws from McArthur prosecution, 135
Benton, Arkansas, 198
Birdcage, 4
BJ's Star Studded Honky Tonk, 5, 58, 59, 73–74, 78, 88, 145, 183, 198
Black Americans for Democracy, 206
Blair, Bobby L., 180
Bomb scare, 214
Bourgeois, 91
Brewer, Beverly, 65–66, 67–68, 73, 80, 81, 83, 86–87
  meets Alice McArthur, 66–67
Brewer, Tom, 65, 66–67, 84, 90, 118
Brown, Darrell F., 206–09
  named special prosecutor, 206–07
  not paid for services, 220
  office break-in, 209
  questions sheriff's tactics, 215–16
  receives threats, 208
Brown, Stan, 211
Browning Arms Company, 77
Bullet hole, 155, 221
Burge, William Larry, 124, 125, 126, 180, 192

admits making phone call, 126
makes "anonymous" phone call,
    121
relationship with Mary "Lee"
    Orsini, 120
testifies at Orsini trial, 158–66
Bynum, George W., 180

Cadaveric spasm, 157
Cajun's Wharf, 68
Capone, Al, 67
Car bomb, 4, 62–63, 76, 77–80,
    89, 98, 137–139, 186
Carnegie Foundation, 206
Carpenter, Claude, 26, 27
Chicago, 40
Christ The King Catholic Church,
    7
CID (see "Criminal Investigation
    Division")
Civil rights lawsuit, 204
    out-of-court settlement, 217–18
Civil Service Commission, 51, 54
Clinton, Arkansas, 20
Clinton, Bill, 55
Colgrove, Al, 65, 85
Colgrove, Karen, 65, 73, 74, 82,
    85, 94
Colorado, 59
Cook, Doyle, 198
Criminal Investigation Division,
    52, 53, 54, 55
Cristoba District of Panama, 206

Davenport, Jack, 23, 24
Dawson, Al, 97, 98, 101, 181, 218
    arrests Mary "Lee" Orsini,
        125–26
    questions Larry Burge about
        phone call, 124
    testifies at Orsini trial, 157
Dental plate, 213
Department of Correction, 55
Department of Public Safety, 55,
    130
Dill, Larry, 60, 94, 95, 96, 97, 98,
    115, 135, 137, 152, 166, 168,
    173, 177, 179, 191, 213, 218
    cited for contempt, 204
    phone conversation with Mary
        "Lee" Orsini, 148–51
    target of civil rights lawsuit, 204

Dillahunty, W. H. "Sonny," 135,
    180, 185
    unpaid for service, 220
Dillard Department Stores, 17, 18
Don T's, 186
Donovan, Tom, 174, 182, 220
"Double whammy," 64
Drugs, 14, 37, 41, 112, 122, 147,
    176–77, 202, 222
Duncan, Oklahoma, 47, 48
Dutton, Diane, 46, 158

Edgar, Rick, 96–97, 98, 100–01,
    212, 218
Edgehill, 4
Editorial, 130
El Patio, 90
Electronic surveillance, 207, 216
Erny, John J., Jr., 178

Farley, T. J., 18, 33, 100
Faubus, Orval, 61
Fayetteville, Arkansas, 22, 50, 180
Federal Bureau of Investigation,
    88, 98
Fifth Amendment, 183, 190
"Florida Chronicle, The," 82
Florida vacation, 81–83
Flowers, 213, 221, 223
    at crime scene, 101
    discrepancy in Hall's accounts,
        147
Foote, William F., 182, 183
Forrest City Police Department,
    109
Fort Polk, Louisiana, 25
"Four Seasons," 65, 68, 72, 73
    "Female Newsletter," 74, 75, 80
    graveside farewell, 118–19
Fowler, Beth, 8, 65, 67–69, 72, 81
    meets Alice McArthur, 67
Fowler, Bob, 65, 66, 68, 84
    fight at Cajun's Wharf, 69
Freedom of Information Act, 216
Freeman, Marty, 198, 202–03
    released, 204
Ft. Walton, Florida, 74

Gachot, Les, 213
Gag order, 129, 134, 176, 202, 217
Glaze, Tom, 33

Golden Meadow, Louisiana, 23, 26, 104
Good old boys, 21, 194
Grand jury, 42, 58, 171, 196, 207, 209, 211, 212, 214, 215, 220
  refuses to indict Bill McArthur, 217
"Great Lipout," 195
Gruber, Rita, 163
Gudmondson, Joyce, 9
  testifies at Orsini trial, 156
Gulf of Mexico, 23

Habeas corpus, 201
"Hale," 88, 89
Hale, David, 135, 176, 182, 184, 197, 202, 220
  binds McArthur over for trial, 193
  issues contempt citations, 203–05
Hale, Jess F. "Doc," 79, 103, 119
  interrogates "Yankee" Hall, 115, 117, 218
  confirms truth of murder tip, 215
  confronted by Tommy Robinson, 147
  relationship with Bill McArthur, 217
Hall, Eugene James "Yankee," 1, 2, 6–7, 100, 109, 110, 112, 114, 115, 117, 126, 136, 171, 177, 180, 185–86, 213, 223
  charged with murder, 116
  implicates Bill McArthur, 117
  may have pulled the trigger, 223
  plea bargains, 131
  pleads guilty, 152
  relationship with Mary "Lee" Orsini, 171–72
  swear statement implicating Orsini, 131
  sworn confession, 137–47
  testifies at Orsini trial, 153–54
Handloser, James, 158
Hardin, John, 54
Harper, Ann, 180
Hatcher Lakes, 12
Hatcher, Frances, 12, 61, 225
Hatcher, Henry, 12, 13
Hatcher, Julia, 12, 13, 16, 221, 225

Hatcher, Mary Myrtle, 11, 13, 14, 15
  (see also "Orsini, Mary 'Lee'")
  marriage to Ronald Orsini, 15
  name change, 15
Hatcher, Ron, 11, 13, 14, 15, 16, 19, 89, 225
  accused of murder, 18
Haynes, Lloyd, 199
Helena, Arkansas, 135
Hensley, Fred, 124, 126, 182, 218
Holt, Jack, Jr., 133, 135, 151, 160, 180, 182, 187, 201, 204, 215, 219
Holt, Joyce, 160
Hot Spring County, 198
Hot Springs, Arkansas, 2, 66, 84, 85, 86, 91, 110, 181, 185
House, Linda, 222
Howard, George, 56
Hypnotist, 182, 183

Jackson, Fletcher, 27
Jacksonville Police Department, 51, 54
Jacksonville, Arkansas, 51, 52, 55
Joe T. Robinson Elementary School, 26
Johnson, Clemmons, 27
Johnson, Paul, 116, 137
Jones, Phoebe, 42, 44, 47, 58, 59, 61, 62
  (see also "Pinkston, Phoebe")
  college, 45
  employed by Bill McArthur, 46
  leaves home, 45–46
  marriage to Paul Pinkston, 62
  plans party for Bill McArthur, 62
  youth, 44
Justice Department, 61

KARN, 194, 195
Kountry Klub Kowboy Disco, 59, 73
KSSN-FM, 59

Lake Hamilton, 66
Lake Hamilton Holiday Inn, 181, 190

Lakewood, 121
Langston, John, 196, 201, 204, 220, 224
   names special prosecutor, 206
Larose, Louisiana, 178
Lassiter, Jack, 45–46, 132, 180, 224
Leroy's Flowers, 160
Lessenberry, Jack, 150, 151, 157, 170, 219
Lester, Jim, 38, 40, 41, 218
   alleges Mary "Lee" Orsini's guilt, 38
   investigation into Orsini murder, 40–42
Lewis, Jim, 53–54
Little Rock Air Force Base, 12, 14, 27, 51, 52
Little Rock Central High School, 193
Little Rock Junior College, 21
Little Rock Police Department, 76, 96, 98, 100, 105, 109, 111, 112, 114, 116, 123, 124, 134, 164, 181, 182, 203, 207–08, 211, 215
   investigation criticized by sheriff, 128–31
   relationship with Pulaski County Sheriff's Department, 98
Little Rock Police Department Intelligence Unit, 216
Lofton, Floyd, 29

Mafia, 80, 109
Malak, Fahmy, 35, 157, 181, 224
Malvern, Arkansas, 198
Mason Jar, 144
Matthews, Wayne, 135
May, David Raymond, 15
McArthur, Alice
   (see also "Miller, Alice")
   body discovered, 95
   children sole heirs of oil lease, 174
   confronts "Ms. X," 31
   first child, 28–29
   Florida vacation plans, 74
   graveside farewell, 117–19
   implicates Bob Troutt in bombing, 78

informs husband about car bomb, 77
   meets Beth Fowler, 67
   meets Beverly Brewer, 67
   murder account, 137–47
   newsletter, 74–76
   oil royalties, 73, 122, 183
   personality, 68, 70
   second child, 28–29
   speculated murder scenario, 223
   takes children to summer camp, 84
McArthur, Billie, 104, 197–98
McArthur, Bryan, 180, 200
McArthur, Chuck, 4, 28, 71, 104, 105, 131–132, 197, 225
McArthur, Robyn, 4, 28, 71, 104, 105, 131–132, 197, 225
McArthur, William C. "Bill"
   accepts mortgage from Mary "Lee" Orsini, 61
   arrested, 132–34
   arrested a second time, 198
   begins law practice, 26
   bound over for trial, 193
   champagne party, 47
   childhood, 20–21
   college, 22–23
   considers opening nightclub, 73
   discovers bullet hole in wall, 92
   employs Phoebe Jones, 45–46
   enters practice with Jack Lassiter, 46
   extramarital affair, 30, 53, 68, 184
   fight at Cajun's Wharf, 69
   files civil rights lawsuit, 204
   first child, 27–28
   first murder trial, 27
   law school, 23–26
   learns of car bomb explosion, 78
   marriage to Alice Miller, 25
   meets Alice Miller, 23
   meets Mary "Lee" Orsini, 33
   meets Tommy Robinson, 51
   news conference, 201
   opens nightclub, 58
   partnership with Floyd Lofton, 29
   pleads innocent, 135
   probable cause hearing, 179–92
   questioned as suspect, 116–17
   realizes wife is dead, 103–04

relationship with Alice, 70
relationship with Jess Hale, 79
retained by Mary "Lee" Orsini, 36
returns home after the murder, 91–92
rumored celebration of wife's death, 118
second child, 28–29
settles civil rights lawsuit, 217–18
suicide rumors, 146–47
takes children to summer camp, 84
testifies at Orsini trial, 167–68
McClellan, John L., 206
McClendon, Larry Darnell, 1, 2, 7, 106, 114, 126, 129, 140–47, 152, 153, 161, 163, 177, 180, 213, 221, 222
convicted of murder, 194
implicated by "Yankee" Hall, 116
named as killer by anonymous caller, 110
McNeely, Robert, 94, 96, 97, 98, 100, 101, 157, 183, 212, 218
Medical examiner, 35, 47, 48
Memphis, Tennessee, 106
Merril the Master Hypnotist, 183
Metropolitan National Bank, 16, 17, 18, 19, 61
Miami Dolphins, 201
"Mike from Malvern," 198
Miles, Buddy, 33
Miller, Alice, 23, 24
(see also "McArthur, Alice")
marriage to Bill McArthur, 26
Miller, Clint, 224
Miller, Leonard, 24, 107, 183
hears Bill McArthur accused, 117–18
Ms. X (pseudonym), 30, 31, 53, 68
testifies at probable cause hearing, 184

Nelson, James, 40, 59, 72, 73, 167, 183, 185
Nelson, Willie, 218
New Orleans, Louisiana, 25, 80, 109
North Little Rock Airport, 60
North Little Rock High School, 50

North Little Rock Police Department, 36, 38, 42, 50, 61, 121, 133–34, 164

Organized crime, 80, 98, 109, 120, 121
Organized Crime and Intelligence Unit, 109
Orsini, Mary "Lee"
(see also "Hatcher, Mary Myrtle")
abandons investigation of husband's death, 61
alleged murder plot at state prison, 175
announces investigation of husband's death, 60
arrested by Little Rock police, 125–26
asks Larry Burge to fake anonymous phone call, 122
champagne party, 47
contrast in appearance, 185
convicted of husband's murder, 223
found guilty of capital murder, 173
grand jury testimony, 211
held for husband's murder, 33
hires private investigator, 38
implicated by "Yankee" Hall's statement, 131
implicated by Hall, 116, 137
invokes Fifth Amendment, 190
involvement in witchcraft alleged, 63–64
not indicted by grand jury, 42
phone conversations with Larry Dill, 148–51
plans party for Bill McArthur, 62
pleads innocent, 126
pleads innocent to capital murder, 153–54
polygraph tests, 40
preferential treatment alleged, 177
prison interview, 212–13
questioned by Little Rock police, 114
receives second mortgage from Bill McArthur, 61
recounts discovering husband's body, 34–35

recounts discovering husband's
body, 34–35
relationship with Larry Burge,
120
rumored celebration of Alice
McArthur's death, 118
serves pie to witnesses, 179
suspected in car bombing, 80
testifies at probable cause
hearing, 181, 185–91
transferred to state prison, 176
trial date set, 126
trial for husband's death
scheduled, 204
weeps under questioning, 42
Orsini, Ronald Gary, 17, 19, 33,
37, 39, 41, 46, 58, 59, 61, 80,
88, 98, 100, 121, 150–51, 171,
192, 204, 222
body discovered, 35
marriage to Mary "Lee"
Hatcher, 15
medical examiner's report, 35
murdered, 18
Orsini, Stacy Renee, 37
Orsini, Tiffany, 18, 35, 41, 49, 58,
64, 149, 151, 170, 173, 223,
225
(see also "Sudbury, Tiffany
LaVergene")
testifies at mother's trial, 171
Our Lady of Prompt Succor
Catholic Church, 25
Ozark Mountains, 21
Ozark, Arkansas, 45

Parkman, Forrest Hamilton, 106,
109, 114, 164, 166, 218
Pawn shop, 62, 102, 105, 108, 158
Piazza, Chris, 64, 107, 126, 147,
153, 155, 166, 168, 170, 172,
175, 194, 219, 224
closing argument at Orsini trial,
171
takes Hall's sworn confession,
137–147
Piggott, Arkansas, 97
Pine Bluff, Arkansas, 135
Pinkston, Paul, 62, 103
Pinkston, Phoebe, 63–64, 77,
84–85, 86, 88, 102, 103, 105,
107, 108, 172, 179, 188, 190,

191, 222
(see also "Jones, Phoebe")
testifies at Orsini trial, 158
Pistol, 128, 139, 171, 181
Plea bargain, 131
Pleasant Valley, 4, 7, 9, 16, 90
Pocahontas, Arkansas, 217
Poinsett County, Arkansas, 109
Pointe Coupee Parish, Louisiana,
73
Polygraph tests, 40
Prather, Anita, 94, 96, 104, 122,
169, 179, 183, 221
discovers Alice McArthur's
body, 94
testifies at Orsini trial, 154–56
Private investigator, 38
Pulaski County, 198
Pulaski County circuit judges, 136
Pulaski County Jail, 126, 137
Pulaski County Sheriff's
Department, 56, 93, 96, 98,
126, 168, 211, 218
Pulaski County, Arkansas, 50, 55
Pulaski Visitors Council, 203
Putman, Bill, 180
Putman, Esther, 180, 192

Radio transmission, 213, 214
Raff, Gene, 135, 150
Regional Organized Crime
Information Center, 106
Reid, J. E., 40
Riverside, California, 14
Robbins, Bob (Robert Spears),
60, 61, 167, 222
Robinson, Tommy F.
alleges Bill McArthur's guilt,
217
announces organized crime
investigation, 79–80
announces Orsini investigation,
60
announces Troutt investigation,
60
arrests Bill McArthur, 199
arrives at crime scene, 98
asks for grand jury, 196
aspirations, 210
cited for contempt, 203–04
confronts Simpson and Hale,
147

continued controversy, 56
continues public comment after
    trial, 175
criticism of investigation,
    129–31
criticized by editorial, 130–31
elected to U.S. House, 219
files subpoenaed by prosecutor,
    128
guest on radio talk show, 193–
    94
jailed by federal judge, 55
meets Bill McArthur, 51
overtures to Darrel Brown,
    207–08
personal history, 50
pressures Darrel Brown, 207
settles civil rights lawsuit,
    217–18
target of civil rights lawsuit, 204
testifies at probable cause
    hearing, 191–92
violates gag order, 203
Rockefeller, Winthrop, 66
Rogers, Opie, 20
Rotary Club, 51, 217
Russellville, Arkansas, 45

Saint Mark's Catholic Church, 23
Saint Vincent Infirmary, 28
Saline County, 198
Shepherd, John, 52–54, 57
Sherwood, Arkansas, 16, 49, 120,
    222
Siegel, Henry, 48
Simpson, Walter F. "Sonny," 99,
    115, 182
    confronted by Tommy Robinson,
        147
Sixth Amendment, 183
"Snow White and the Seven
    Dwarfs," 71–72
Southwestern Bell Telephone
    Company, 158–59
Soviet Union, 56
Spears, Robert (Bob Robbins),
    59, 60, 167, 222
Special prosecutor, 135, 180, 206,
    215, 219, 221
Special Weapons and Tactics
    team, 54–55
Springdale, Arkansas, 130

St. Louis, Missouri, 48
Starr, John Robert, 123, 195, 200
State Rehabilitation Department,
    23
Statute 43–1414, 201
"Sting," 212
Sudbury, Douglas, 14
Sudbury, Tiffany LaVergene, 14,
    15
    (see also "Orsini, Tiffany")
"Sun Day," 76
Super Bowl Sunday, 197
Superior Federal Savings, 17
SWAT team (see "Special Weapons
    and Tactics team")
Swayze, Michael, 197, 198, 202–
    03, 204
Sweet potato pies, 179

Telephone trap, 6, 60, 158, 172
"Three Musketeers," 67
Troutt, Bob, 59, 61, 62, 73, 80,
    98, 100, 106, 113, 122, 144,
    160, 164, 180, 183, 215, 222
    arrested, 61
    implicated in car bombing, 78
Troutt, Holly, 106, 163, 164, 165
Tumbleweed, 168
Tuscaloosa Trend, 73

U.S. Pizza Company, 190
Union Bank Building, 209
United States Attorney, 135
United States Marshal's Service,
    50
United States Supreme Court, 224
University of Arkansas, 21, 50
University of Arkansas at Little
    Rock, 14, 51
University of Arkansas School of
    Law, 206
University of Southwestern
    Louisiana, 25

Videotapes, 199, 201

Waggoner, Tom, 132
Walls, John, 90
Walls, Peggy, 65, 85, 90
Washington Redskins, 201
Washington University, 48

Westchester County, New York, 48

Westside Tennis & Fitness Club, 3

Williams, Bill, 112, 116

Williams, Randall, 152, 173, 175, 176

Williamson, Reed, 51

Willingham, Mike, 7, 110, 111–12, 140, 166, 218

Wilson, Carl, 154, 186

Wine Cellar, 15

Witchcraft, 64

Wolf, Tery, 152

Woodward, Bobby, 52, 53, 56, 97, 199, 211, 219
  presence at murder scene, 212
  takes Bill McArthur into custody, 133–135

Wulz, Ann, 47, 48–49

Wulz, Charles F., 36, 48, 49, 58, 59, 121, 125, 139, 160, 164, 172, 177, 221
  acquitted of wife's murder, 46–48
  champagne party, 47
  charged with wife's murder, 47
  moves to Arkansas, 48
  personal history, 47–48
  pistol missing, 128–29
  relationship with Mary "Lee" Orsini, 171
  summoned to prosecutor's office, 175
  testifies at Orsini trial, 171–72

Wulz, Claudia, 49

Wulz, Tamara, 47, 172

Younts, Bill, 120, 164